Additional Praise for *Offerings of the Heart*

"Shawn Zevit is a master at guiding people towards a values-based approach to money and wealth in congregational life. This book now brings that wisdom to a wider audience. Read it and get a glimpse of the possibilities of creating true communities of faith."
—Rabbi Sid Schwarz, founder and president, PANIM: The Institute for Jewish Leadership and Values.

"Most of us who care about congregations think about money as a necessary evil—a distasteful medium we are required to deal with so we can pay the bills of the institution. Focusing on generosity, Rabbi Shawn Zevit has gathered much of the wisdom of the Jewish community learned through four millennia of life with God. He shows us the rich thought and experience Hebrew scriptures and traditions contribute for all who seek to be faithful in the use of money in their communities. A deep understanding of generosity and giving is brought to bear on the practicalities of budgets, planning, and reaching out in deeds of justice and mercy. Zevit has provided a remarkable resource for us all."
—Loren B. Mead, founder, the Alban Institute

"Our world is driven by greed and cut-throat capitalism. Our politicians profess Biblical values but are more influenced by money than morality when making decisions. At such a time, how do synagogues and churches raise money, use money, and teach about money? In this wonderful book, Rabbi Zevit helps us to answer this question by weaving together traditional and contemporary Jewish texts, history, practical advice, and real-world examples. I highly recommend it."
—Rabbi Eric H. Yoffie, president, Union for Reform Judaism

"Money is neither the root of all evil nor the sum and substance of all good. In itself, money is morally neutral. How one acquires and uses it, however, raises many moral questions. Many of us are familiar with those issues as individuals, but how do we handle money morally as leaders of institutions? Zevit shows us how Judaism guides us in such matters. He discusses ample and clearly explained traditional sources and offers helpful suggestions and exercises demonstrating how to apply them to modern circumstances."
—Rabbi Elliot N. Dorff, author of *To Do the Right and the Good: A Jewish Approach to Modern Social Ethics*

"This book can serve as a useful resource for synagogues grappling with a variety of monetary issues, from planning and budgeting to membership development and capital campaigns. Rather than dictating a particular approach, Rabbi Zevit teases out the issues, offers a variety of relevant texts, and presents case studies and sample exercises from contemporary congregations."
—Isa Aron, professor of Jewish Education, Rhea Hirsch School of Education

D1051256

"Fundraising—a soul-raising, community-building activity—"organizes" money that already exists. As signs of covenant and commitment, money gifts are spiritual tools that link budgets with mission and vision-driven planning. Zevit's systems approach in *Offerings of the Heart*, relating money decisions to identity and values, will be taken seriously in Canadian faith communities."
—Barbara Fullerton, stewardship development officer, the United Church of Canada

"Amid the noise of commercialism that beckons us to purchase an array of items comes insightful guidance from the deepest recesses of the Jewish psyche. Rabbi Shawn Zevit has brought together much wisdom in this practical volume, which has one clear and straightforward message: we should be spending money for a purpose—to serve the needs of others and not merely to glorify the self."
—Rabbi Kerry M. Olitzky, executive director, the Jewish Outreach Institute

"*Offerings of the Heart* explores the critical interrelationship of spirituality, community, and ethical issues concerning money. Combining classical religious texts, contemporary examples, and exercises that every congregation can use, Rabbi Shawn Zevit shows how a covenantal community should deal with its income and expenses. Readers will learn in practical terms how communities can bring their values to bear on how they handle their congregations' financial life. For congregational leaders, reading this book will be an eye-opener that leads to concrete action."
—Rabbi David A. Teutsch, author of *Spiritual Community: The Power to Restore Hope, Commitment and Joy*

"In millennia past, Jews who had little money learned how to provide for their own struggling families while sharing with the hard-pressed community as a whole. Now, when Jewish communities are often well-off and the broader economy is much more complex, the question is how to use that wealth responsibly and wisely. Rabbi Zevit draws on the rich wisdom of the past while creatively teaching us how to work out new Jewish understandings about money for the future."
—Rabbi Arthur Waskow, director, the Shalom Center

"Rabbi Zevit brings a refreshing and insightful approach to one of the most challenging areas of our personal and congregational life—money and faith. His presentation of rabbinic sources, from the early days of Exodus through modern musings, provides new foundational teachings for those of us who have struggled with this money journey. The practical exercises open the way for the movement of the Spirit in congregations bold enough to honestly engage in the experience of group assessment and growth. Congregations from all faiths and denominations will benefit greatly from this book."
—Kevin Cashman, director, Ministry of Money

OFFERINGS OF THE HEART

OFFERINGS OF THE HEART

Money and Values in Faith Communities

RABBI SHAWN ISRAEL ZEVIT

THE
ALBAN
INSTITUTE

Herndon, Virginia
www.alban.org

The Alban Institute
2121 Cooperative Way, Suite 100
Herndon, VA 20171-5370

Cover design by Adele Robey, Phoenix Graphics.

Library of Congress Cataloging-in-Publication Data

Zevit, Shawn Israel.
  Offerings of the heart : money and values in faith communities / Shawn Israel Zevit.
      p. cm.
  Includes bibliographical references.
  ISBN 1-56699-281-8
  1. Money—Religious aspects—Judaism. 2. Charity—Religious aspects—Judaism. 3. Jewish ethics. I. Title.

BM538.M66Z48 2005
296.6'5—dc22
                                        2005016445

  10   09   08   07   06   05   BM   1   2   3   4   5   6

CONTENTS

Foreword

A rabbi who was intent on fostering his congregants' relationship with God was asked, "Rabbi, how can we think of God while we are doing business?" The rabbi responded, "You think of business while you are praying, so you can think of God while you are doing business."

How much more, when we are doing the business of our congregations, do we need to think about God. Rabbi Shawn Zevit has given us a manual for doing just that.

Most congregational boards spend more time discussing issues related to money than anything else. In a parallel universe, money is the most frequent subject of biblical commandments, teachings, and parables. But rare is the congregation board that makes a connection between these two worlds. As a result, boards' decisions about money are frequently not informed by the values they profess. Here is a valuable teaching moment about the relevance of religious values to the decisions we make about money.

We live in a society where money is glorified, where many people judge their own and others' self-worth by how much money they have, and where money connotes power. No wonder it is difficult to have honest conversations about money in our congregations. It is often said by sociologists and therapists that most people would rather tell you intimate details about their sex lives than tell you how much money they have in the bank. A congregation that can create a safe place to talk about money has made a significant step towards creating a holy community.

Healthy congregations seek to build sacred community. Running a congregation requires dealing with money—collecting and allocating resources—and although many attempt to deny it, there is no way around this reality. Therefore, we need to learn how to infuse our financial decision making with a consciousness of God. Rabbi Zevit has provided us with a methodology and tools to bring God into the business of the congregation.

The beauty of this book is that Rabbi Zevit opens his heart to us by sharing his own feelings and thoughts about money while at the same time giving us very practical steps about how congregations can learn to incorporate religious values into all levels of their relationship to money. His very method of presentation models the various sensibilities that a congregation needs to bring to its financial decisions. He writes in a personal style, anchored in his relationship to God, and offers a values-based approach based on traditional texts. He addresses the concrete work of a congregation making decisions about dues, organizing money (i.e., raising funds), and budgeting for priorities.

In my twenty years of congregational consulting, I have often observed how a congregation's myths and stories obscure issues about resource collection and allocation. As living organisms, congregations change throughout their lives, and frequently stories about the past prevent them from developing an accurate perception of who they are now. I once worked with a congregation that prided itself on its level of Jewish knowledge and the quality of their adult education programs. That "golden age" had occurred 20 years prior, but a careful examination showed that during the time we worked together, the congregation allocated minimal resources to adult education and a majority of the congregants were brought up with little or no Jewish education. Engaging in the visioning, values, and mission exercises in this volume will help readers uncover the myths of their congregations and allocate resources to match congregational needs.

This book can be used by congregations of all faiths, even though it is told from a Jewish perspective. Years of congregational research has shown that congregational dynamics are very similar, regardless of denomination. All congregations deal with money and budgets, all try to root their decisions in their faith, and all congregational boards operate in similar fashions. Yet I think it is of particular importance for Christians to learn about Jewish values regarding money. Despite years of sincere work on the part of significant numbers of Christian clergy and laity, centuries of anti-Semitic stereotypes about Jews and money still live in our culture. In fact on the day that I write this, a student in one of my classes recounted the following:

Several years ago, while playing on a sports team at an affluent Northeast suburban high school, a teammate made a remark about "Jewing someone down." My student remarked that it was an offensive phrase. The following day, during a game, the teammate began pitching pennies at her while saying, "You're a Jew! Don't you want to pick them up?"

A deeper understanding of Jewish values about money will help Christian leaders educate others and counter anti-Semitic stereotypes. Studying Jewish values about taking care of the poor and tithing will give Christians a better understanding of the deep connections between Judaism and Christianity.

The Bible teaches us that the job of human beings is to be responsible stewards of the earth's resources and that as such we are God's partners. Responsible stewardship of resources is the guiding principle of every congregational board. Far too often responsibility is understood as keeping things the way they are, not making changes, not taking risks. Congregational leaders sometimes need to take risks, and at times, the responsible choice is to experiment with a new program. Sometimes, however, leaders need to stop and ask, "To whom are we responsible?"

A traveling preacher once arrived in a town and proceeded to teach at the synagogue. One man asked him, "Who do you work for?" The preacher hired that man to be his traveling companion for one purpose: to ask him throughout the day, "Who do you work for?" By examining our values and our hearts, we remember what the work of our congregations is really about.

Offerings of the Heart: Money and Values in Faith Communities is a unique and important book. The title conveys the synthesis that it achieves. It brings together the four realms of existence: the practical (money), the emotional (heart), the intellectual (values), and the spiritual (faith). Reading the text and then engaging in the study and exercises found in each chapter could transform congregations. It will help everyone become a partner to God in the work of building congregational community.

Rabbi Mordechai Liebling
Torah of Money Director
The Shefa Fund

PREFACE

And everyone who excelled in ability and everyone whose
spirit moved them . . . all the men and women whose hearts
moved them to bring anything for the work that God,
through Moses, had commanded to be done, brought it as a
freewill offering to God.

—Exod. 35:21, 29

Dearest Source of Life
You are in us as a longing for each other
You are in us as a striving for Self
"Build for Me a sacred dwelling place
And I will dwell among you" the Torah states
And so the longing that is the I
And the longing that is the We
Come together in holy endeavor
To create a life and a home
Where the resources we are blessed with
Great or small, temporary or ongoing
Are directed and organized with an open heart
That You may dwell in the space within and between us.
As we journey through these pages
May we bring You home
In the flow of our resources
In our hearts and through our hands.

—Shawn Zevit, 2005/5765

In the Beginning

As I began the journey of writing this book, asking for God's direction in the opportunity and privilege to do so, I experienced the excitement and awesome possibility of bringing Jewish wisdom about money to those who have made building religious community and communal organizations their volunteer or professional life. I also experienced anxiety, a sense of inadequacy, and blocks to bringing a sacred approach to money in my own life. I know I am not alone in this, for you are sharing these words with me, drawn by your own curiosity or need. I have yet to meet anyone, no matter how solid their faith, that is free of struggle when it comes to dollars and "sense." And so the journey begins, and the gates of inquiry open.

The longing to engage life from a perspective of abundance and faith, not scarcity and fear, is also at the heart of my inquiry into this subject. It reflects my passion and commitment to bringing the depth and breadth of Jewish teachings on money and spiritual life to all faith communities, given the central role finances have in our world. It has also been a painful struggle at times to write on a subject that has asked me to enter into long-held fears of the presence and absence of money in my life. I have needed to explore feelings of self-worth, tied to what we see is "of worth" in our world. The fact that it is easier in many of our faith communities to talk about spirituality or sexuality than how much we earn or spend personally, and how money is organized in our congregations, added to the challenge in writing *Offerings of the Heart*.

Images from my childhood—the place where so many foundational attitudes about money were set in motion—come flooding in. Flashes of my life growing up as a second-generation middle-class Canadian Jew in Winnipeg, Manitoba, and later in Toronto, Ontario, come to mind. I share these early memories with you as an invitation to recall your own formative experiences with money and values from your own traditions, and how they impact your choices and attitudes around money today.

At first, I see a *pushka* (charitable collection box) being circulated around my classroom in the 1960s to gather pennies for planting trees in Israel. There's another paper box to collect change for the United Nations program for children in need, and a third sitting at my grandparents for new immigrant funds. Everywhere, in Jewish settings, these little boxes for Jewish and larger world causes greeted my comings and goings. Unless they were old pennies of value to me, a burgeoning collector of stamps and coins, these "coppers" were to be collected and deposited for those who did not have the opportunity to do the same.

These pennies, with either Queen Elizabeth or Abraham Lincoln on them, pop up at Jewish holidays too. My family gathered for Hanukkah, the celebration of political and religious freedom that the Maccabees won for the Jewish people over 2,000 years ago, and spun the *dreidel* (a top with four Hebrew letters on it that stand for a "great miracle happened there"). I can visualize the scene. Everyone antes up a penny, and depending on which letter the top falls on, we get a penny or give a penny, take the pot or just half of it. Jelly beans or peanuts will suffice in the absence of coins, but shrieks of delight and shouts of desired outcomes fill the air. At evening's end, we say goodnight to my great-grandfather Ben Zion and my grandparents, half the booty given to the omnipresent *tzedakah* (charitable giving) box, half for our own collection. I learned early on that our "winnings" are never just ours. There is always someplace where those in need can benefit, even from our meager take.

Passage into adult membership in Jewish community is marked by the bar mitzvah (for boys) and the bat mitzvah (for girls). It recognizes that the young person has reached the age of responsibility for one's own Jewish practice and welcomes the 13-year-old as an adult in the Jewish community. There is the process of learning, preparing, and reciting a portion of the Torah in public. Surrounding my particular bar mitzvah is a lunch at the synagogue and a gathering back at my parents' home for friends and family that night. A few gifts of Judaica, books, Canadian and Israeli bonds arrive. The impression I am most left with is the meaning system attached to the gifts, usually given in increments of 18 or 36 dollars. As each Hebrew letter has a numerical value, and the word *chai* (life) has a numerical value of eighteen, blessings for life and double life are expressed. Money is not just for "things," but also for enhancing and bringing meaning to life itself.

To this day, whenever I make a charitable contribution that does not list a multiple of 18 as an option, I check the "other" box and write in my own variation of a *chai* donation. My accompanying prayer is, "You who receive this offering, may it enhance your life, and the life of those who receive from you." Money is both an actual and symbolic tool for the deepening and sustaining of life, and through its giving and receiving, we can inspire others and be inspired ourselves. We can align ourselves with the values we hold and those we reach for.

Later in my teenage years came what I fondly term "Fund-raising 101"—the United Jewish Appeal walks for Israel. The dollars-per-mile forms are circulated in the class, and we gather pledges and show up for the hike across a dozen or more miles in Toronto. Regardless of who has gathered the pledge, this seems to be a family or pack-of-friends event. We are walking in public as a community, but not only for our community. I feel exposed and vulnerable, proud and excited. This is repeated over time in walks for cancer and AIDS research. Marching collectively as a Jew in public is tied in my memory to raising consciousness and raising money for a cause.

My memories of money are not all silver-lined. Growing up, money was at times available and at other times scarce. Many of the heated discussions I remember were forged in the gulf between what was desired or expected as part of the North American dream of upward mobility, and what was possible given the limitations of financial resources. Money was generously given to those who needed it, and at the same time a source of conflict and need. Issues of class also existed, and still do, under the radar screen, but were a felt presence at the kitchen table on many occasions.

Money was also a mystery. How does it work? How is it managed? Why do some people have more than others? How do you save or spend it wisely? These were not explicit conversations at home, school, or even my first jobs. Money seemed to exist independently of us, influencing choices of generosity or selfishness, compassion or cruelty. I remember once lying to a teacher of mine in the 1960s—that we had one of the "new" color televisions at home, which my parents brought to my attention after it was mentioned to them in casual conversation at a parent-teacher interview at my school. It seems that in making conversation with my parents, my teacher congratulated them on their new purchase—itself an interesting subject for her to focus on. The fact was we had a fine black-and-white television. I do not consciously remember the forces at work that led me to conjure up this possession, but I do remember the embarrassment I felt when I was caught and my mother's compassion and kind urging that I need not make things up to "fit in." Yet the unspoken pressures of class and status in the world around me had begun to seep in.

Power, status, and wealth all contribute to this definition of class and, depending on one's frame of reference, the felt abundance or scarcity of resources. This is a particularly sensitive area in the Jewish community, where exclusion from the larger culture forced many Jews to make it on their own in some entrepreneurial way. Being predominantly white in a white majority culture allowed for access that people of color were often denied, yet being Jewish closed a whole host of other doors. These issues of class and race were (and are) often so subtle and complex as to defy identification and discussion, yet they are present in all areas of money and communal life.

There were societal images of Jews and money that gave rise to anti-Semitic comments I would hear. This implicit and explicit prejudice spurred my grandparents and parents to find their own way in the world and extend a loan or a job to those in need. Memories abound of my father giving jobs to new immigrants who spoke no English to help them get settled. Later, when I worked for a decade with a small educational theater company in Toronto, most often at the poverty line in wages, I never felt that I was lacking anything, as long as I had meaningful work. I also came to realize that I had issues to overcome in asking for compensation. It was as if I felt I could not live according to God's ways if I were paid a livable wage. I would break into a sweat when I asked for a reasonable daily fee for consultation services or negotiated a salary increase, yet I never questioned what I was giving to charitable causes. Part of the ongoing work I have needed to do as an adult in this area is to be aware of how money is linked to self-esteem, religion, class, and power dynamics in relationships. Later, through life as a parent and partner, I have come to acknowledge that the higher goal of meaningful work and compensation needs to be balanced with practical demands and needs. The desire to balance this practical demand with core personal values is an ongoing challenge. In many ways I find this mirrored on the communal level as congregations struggle with the relationship between their missions and their budgets.

There is a Jewish tradition, rooted in the Hebrew Bible, to tithe one's income or produce to benefit others.[1] Even one who was the beneficiary of such righteous giving still needed to tithe what they received. This imperative (mitzvah) encourages us to find a way to help, even when our own resources are limited. No matter what one's own need at the moment, there is always someone who is in greater need, and the definition of want and need is subject to higher values of justice in the allocation of resources.

Years later I found myself, as both an independent consultant and congregational consultant for the Jewish Reconstructionist

Federation, in the role of a resource, trainer, and program delivery person to organizations and congregations around North America. Money and congregational life became a prime area of consultative need and service delivery wherever I turned. It is a journey that brought me into contact with Rabbi Mordechai Liebling, Jeffery Dekro, the Alban Institute, and to this project today.

These are but a small set of snapshots from the album of my influential memories. We all have them. Often we may not even be aware as to how these lessons of family and faith come to guide our sermon from the pulpit, our budgeting comments at the board meeting, our direction of congregational programming, spending, or charitable giving. For some faith communities and organizations, core religious teachings on financial and human resources may be front and center in the system. For others, values may be implicit in the approaches to revenue and expenditure, or they may have become separated from bottom-line financial decision making, lost in the quest for balanced budgets and repairing leaky roofs.

Confusion or tension can also exist between private financial practices and faith-based congregational practices, or between religious values and traditions and the business aspects of running a congregation or organization. Our contemporary world does not ask us to put our financial practices through a religious audit to see how our actions line up with living a godly life. Simply attending synagogue, mosque, church, or meeting place does not, in and of itself, heal this divide. We must also consider what spiritual insights might guide and determine our choices within the sanctuary, and how the prayers and policies of our congregations contribute to us all living lives *b'tzelem Elohim*—in the image of God.[2]

A Theological Note

Our religious heritages provide a wide spectrum of thought about God and how God is present in our lives. The positive or negative experiences and concepts you had about God growing up may be the greatest influence on you today, or you may have undergone profound changes from the beliefs you grew up with. For some of you the Scriptures (including the rabbinic texts if you are Jewish) may be seen as the literal word of God given at Sinai. For others among you these may be textual records of humanity's quest for God or for a life guided by humanity's sacred principles that spread across the centuries. Still others of you may uphold certain values and religious practices but struggle with any formal concept or belief in God. You may have already experienced shifts in your theological viewpoint and spiritual practice, depending on your experience, religious upbringing, or stage of life.

Whether you experience and understand God as working through human agency or personally directing the course of individual human events, as a personal being or as a force in the universe, or whether you struggle with the very existence of a divinity, your conception of the principles of your faith tradition are bound to affect and be reflected in your attitudes towards money and in your making and spending of it.

When we gather in congregational settings, we come with our individual beliefs and interact with communal policies, customs, and practices. Likewise, the belief and behavior systems in our faith communities influence who we become and how we think about critical issues such as financial and human resources. We may ask ourselves: What core values inform our decision making? How do God, tradition, *halakhah* (literally "a way" or Jewish religious law and teachings), and our core values inform our decisions around money in our congregations or organizations?

At times differences between individual values and beliefs and those of our religions can be mutually enhancing, and at other times they may be in tension. We can benefit greatly in our communication and choices about financial matters when we share not only balance sheets but concerns over how money is connected to our theologies, deeply held values, and life experience. Avoiding these discussions—viewing them as "not related to the bottom line" or relegating God-talk or values clarification to moments deemed spiritual—contributes to a financial and spiritual split where we may consider our financial decision making as unrelated to us being the best person or community of faith we can be.

From a Jewish perspective, this is not a new philosophy. The view that money is a tool for doing God's work, or put another way, embodying godliness in our deeds, is present from the time of Abraham's interactions with neighboring Canaanite peoples through the birth of the Jewish people in the exodus from Egypt, up to the present day. It is this sense of stewardship of Divine resources, and of values-based decision making in all areas of congregational life, including finances, that informs our conversation in *Offerings of the Heart*.

A Brief Historical Note

As part of this preface I wanted to briefly touch on some historical stages in the development of the Jewish people and the relationship to financial resources. At the very birth of the Jewish people in the exodus from Egypt, Jews traditionally paid a minimum tax to support the establishment and maintenance of their ritual sacred center (the Tent of Meeting or *ohel mo'ed* in the desert), their leadership, and later the Temples *(Bet HaMikdash)* where the priests made their sacrifices. They also provided a share of their tribal allocation to the Levites so that the Levites could focus on the needs of the sacrificial cult. Thus there was an obligatory contribution to support *avodah* (sacred service).

There were a variety of avenues developed for expressing thanks for the blessings attributed to God-given bounty in the fields and the home. Some of these ways of expressing thanks also provided the disenfranchised or stranger to Israelite society with sustenance. The land itself had to be given a rest every seven years *(shemitah)* and every fiftieth year was deemed a jubilee or *yovel* where all debts were forgiven and possessions were returned to their original owners (though scholars disagree as to how or whether this was ever actualized). A portion of each field was left to those in need, and there was the practice of tithing a percentage of one's produce for one's own celebration of abundance, for those in need and for the Temple. All these were based on the perspective that the earth and natural resources are God's, and that sustenance, land, and wealth are Divine gifts we are to steward. The prophetic critique of religious, social, economic, and political inequality and inequities at different times in the Bible may challenge an assumption that these ideals were lived up to with regularity. However, they are clearly presented as an ideal and a mark of economic justice to be measured against everyday actions.

As Rabbinic Judaism developed from 200 BCE onwards, the rabbis helped systematize the flow and allocation of resources by promoting and enshrining in law core values of holiness, community building, compassionate action, and service to God. The Jewish spirit of practicality in religious life is expressed in the rabbinic saying, "Where there is no bread, there can be no Torah, Where there is no Torah, There will be no bread" ("Pirket Avot"/Ethics of the Sages, 3:17).

In the middle ages the *parnaseem* (community leaders)[3] were often asked to raise taxes for the government and they also developed a process to charge a Jewish communal tax for the maintenance of religious institutions, as well as *tzedekah* (giving for just and compassionate ends)[4] for the widow, orphan, and all those in need. Jewish law and custom kept pace with ongoing interpretations of past biblical and Talmudic *halakhah*[5] to meet different situations as Jews found themselves in new societies due to the expulsion from one or the invitation to join another. Jews also followed emerging trade routes due in large part to their not being allowed to own land in many places, and limits on their being able to participate in professional trades and guilds.

The rise of the modern nation-state and the option in some countries for Jews to become citizens of those states opened up new opportunities to be engaged in economic life. This brought new possibilities and also awakened long-standing prejudices. Institutions and methods built on biblical and rabbinic foundations continued to develop in these modern nation-states, whereby money could be distributed by guilds or groups to those in need and collected for Jewish communal activities. Some of these groups included *kibbutzim* in Israel, especially after the founding of the modern state in 1948, international relief organizations to aid Jewish communities in need or to enable Jews to leave places of persecution, and Jewish welfare agencies in Canada and the United States in particular. The establishment of the synagogue, and later Jewish agencies and community centers in North America, also led to new areas of fundraising and financial distribution.

In North America, a key part of Jewish identification and sense of belonging became connected to membership in synagogues of a variety of developing Jewish movements—Orthodox streams, Reform (late 1800s), Conservative (early 1900s), Reconstructionist (1950s), Jewish Renewal and the Havurah Network (1960s)—and a variety of smaller and developing streams of Jewish life. The synagogue continues to remain central to Jewish communal life, but the involvement by Jews in institutions outside the Jewish community also increased as religious and ethnic barriers began to fall after the Second World War. This has meant that resources once directed internally within the Jewish community are now also directed outside as well. This holds true for all faith-based organizations today, which have to compete with multiple volunteer options and worthwhile causes available to their memberships outside a particular religious denomination, congregation, or ethnic community.

The synagogue of today has considerably more extensive financial needs than before. It has taken on many other functions that the old synagogue was not solely responsible for. It is a *beit midrash* (a school for adult and child learning), a *beit knesset* (a house of assembly), a social center (a site for meetings, celebratory dinners and events, and so forth), a social service center (where life-cycle events, pastoral counseling, day care, and so forth take place), a cultural center, a youth center, and so on. The cost of infrastructure, salaries, and programming to meet these diverse needs has become substantial. At the same time, the yearning to belong to a faith community and the choice to learn, grow, and express oneself as a Jew, or in partnership with someone who is Jewish, has found a renaissance in North America.

THE GOALS OF THIS BOOK

Ideally and historically, the Jewish people have been committed to looking at financial resources as tools for building sacred community, reflecting the Divine image in the very structures and foundations of communal life. The foundational approach to economic resources from biblical times onwards has been to operate within available resources and to thank God by offering back a portion of what we have been graced with.

In today's parlance, money is an expression of the values we are actually committed to in our actions as well as the commitments we hold internally to do godly action in the world. Budgets and spending priorities become a reflection of our priorities, which in turn reflect the values articulated by a communal mission statement supported by the entire community.

In his book *Judaism as a Civilization*,[6] Rabbi Mordecai Kaplan, founder of Reconstructionist Judaism, expressed the idea that Judaism is more than a religion. It is the evolving religious civilization of the Jewish people. This includes rituals, liturgies, and religious practices, as well as art, dress, language, ethnicity, and so on. For most of Jewish history, religious belief and behavior tended to define a person's sense of belonging in their community. Nowadays, it is often an individual's feeling part of something larger than themselves, in alignment with a personal need or spiritual journey, that tends to determine whether they will attach themselves to a congregation, organization, or belief system. Oftentimes, a flashpoint for the sense of belonging and identity is most pronounced where financial commitment and the process of fund-raising and spending arise in faith-based community.

In congregations, we are also pulled in a variety of directions that, on the surface, can seem in opposition to the very foundations of our endeavor. We are neither for-profit "businesses" in the marketplace, nor classic nonprofit organizations. We have dimensions of both, with the added ingredient of a spiritual and culturally-based mission. I like to think of our faith-based communities as "for-prophet enterprises," sharing the ultimate goals of manifesting the sacred values, laws, and cultural traditions we have come to hold dear.

This book asks us to examine our prevailing attitudes and behaviors around money and religious life in community and in our own hearts, with a goal of transforming and inspiring our thought and action around money. This book also aims at providing texts, tools, and contemporary approaches to help clergy, staff, and lay leadership of congregations and organizations of any faith in approaching financial resources as core means to building and maintaining whole and holy lives in a communal setting. The sacred mission of religious organizations raises the questions that relate to this goal—how our communities can create *conscious* values-based approaches to developing and managing financial and human resources, rooted in the very sacred traditions, principles, and impulses that brought us together. Values-based decision making is something that most communities or organizations do in an unself-conscious way. In many cases it is marketplace values that are the driving force. It's not that people don't have values or use them. Religious values are often different from marketplace values, so by employing them consciously, we will end up with different decisions.

As congregations and religious organizations struggle with these questions, they must also address concrete, new, and ongoing needs, which include staffing, physical space, prayer books, youth and adult education programs, social justice and human support programs, ritual items, and so much more. The path to dealing with these issues from a spiritual perspective begins with a personal dimension. It is important, for example, to overcome the various stigmas in our society concerning money, while at the same time acknowledging our own discomfort levels.

First, we need to create a trusting environment for such a discussion. Conversations about money in a communal setting can be challenging, because issues of class and money are tied to issues of self-worth, personal values, and individual choices. We may have discomfort or even shame at having too much, too little, or not enough. Envy, competition, and insecurity can all surface when we talk about financial issues. The intensity of discussion, opinion, and emotion can increase when attached to conversations about religion and religious and ethnic identity, especially when there has been little in the way of education and dialogue about money and religious life. Through study, effective listening, and open discussion of our attitudes and expectations, however, we can turn a potentially challenging subject into a profound opportunity for building relationships and community.

There has never been any organized religion that did not need resources of some kind, expecting its members to contribute offerings, dues, or taxes to support its institutions. Along with the personal dimension as described above, we need to develop workable congregational systems where funds are collected and managed in a fair and just manner that both reflects our values and inspires further giving.

While the approach taken is rooted in the experience and insights that have evolved over 3,000 years of the Jewish people's journey, it can be applied to any congregation or organization. There may be different creative ways of answering the same questions depending on the size and life cycle of a community, the professional and lay leadership involved, and the resources on hand. Looking at money in a faith-based communal setting does mean asking that we view our responses through a certain lens that may effectively deepen and change who we are and how we respond to a given issue. Outcomes and financial plans are a necessity. So is examining the basis for our decisions and the way we arrive at them.

This is not a comprehensive book on how to do budgets and capital campaigns, spend or save money. There are more expert materials on these subject areas available from the Alban Institute, the synagogue and church movements, Jewish federations, denominations of all faiths, and the nonprofit and business worlds; however, this is a foundational book about some Jewish values-based approaches to the multiple streams through which financial concerns run in our congregations. While the focus will be congregational life, the approaches and issues we explore also apply to the use of money in any community of faith and the larger culture we live in. We will explore a variety of approaches to a given subject, using traditional Jewish and contemporary sources. We will look at best practices from congregational life and at ways to educate and inspire our home communities to incorporate these ideas whatever our religious tradition. We will examine the development of these attitudes and *halakhot* as they pertain to our missions, plans, budgets, fund-raising campaigns, and giving.

One of the Hebrew words most known to the world is *shalom*. Hebrew is a meaning-laden language, initially constructed around two- or three-letter root words from which all concepts are expressed. The word *shalom* (peace, hello, good-bye) comes from the word *shalem* (wholeness or completeness). In a wonderful embodiment of a Jewish approach to the Divine and human intersecting in the world of practical matters, the word for paying for an item to take possession of it became *l'shalem*. To obtain something is to create an exchange that leaves all parties feeling whole and holy in their comings and goings with each other. Money used as a spiritual tool in this way has the potential to leave everyone resting in a place of peace, of *shalom*.

The goal in Jewish tradition of approaching money through this spiritual consciousness is not only peaceful transactions, but also the development of an ethical human being reflecting God in fundamental actions where heaven and earth intersect. Moses Maimonides, one of the most prolific and influential medieval Jewish leaders and known also by his acronym "the RaMBaM," writes:

> The commerce of the learned person has to be in truth and in faith. Their yes is to be yes and their no, no; they force themselves to be exact in calculations when they are paying, but are willing to be lenient to their debtors. One is not to buy on credit when one has the wherewithal to pay cash. . . . One should keep one's word in commerce, even where the laws allow them to withdraw or retract, so that their word is their bond. . . . One should be careful not to deprive one's neighbor of their livelihood or cause anguish or hardship to others. One who does all these things is the one referred to by the prophet Isaiah, when he said, "You, Israel, are My servant, with whom I am exalted."[7]

As you dip lightly or deeply into these chapters, may the offerings of your own heart be stirred so that you and your treasured communities can live into all you are and are yet to be. Imagine a world in which our religious institutions and networks of sacred relationships stand as an inspiration and practical example for a global community operating in the image of the Divine. Envision how you and your congregation, organization, or community's actions could be active participants in this goal. Money, how it is organized and viewed, is an integral part of realizing this dream.

ACKNOWLEDGMENTS

The materials that went into this book and the thinking that underlies it are the products of dozens of conversations, interactions, and
learning experiences with many dedicated people. People generously
gave of their time, sifted through their written materials and communications, and provided the creative input that helped me develop this resource on money and Jewish values.

I am indebted to my dear friend and colleague Rabbi Mordechai
Liebling of the Shefa Fund; to Jeffery Dekro, executive director of
the Shefa Fund; and to Rabbi Toba Spitzer of Dorshei Tzedek in
Newton, Massachusetts, for all of their groundbreaking work in the
area of money and Jewish values and their contributions to this book;
to Rabbi Jonathan Malamy, Anna Rosenfeld, and Rabbi Rena
Blumenthal for their assistance and research in my earlier work in
the area of money and Jewish values.

I thank Beth Ann Gaede, my ever-supportive editor, and the
staff at the Alban Institute for their patience and faith in my ability
to realize this project. Special thanks to Lilly Endowment Inc. for its
grant towards the writing of this book.

I am deeply grateful to my wife, Talia Malka, my stepson Elia
Malka, my parents Les and Sheila Zevit, my sister Pamela Zevit, and
in-laws Leah and Milt Mandelblatt (may his memory be for a blessing); friends and teachers Paul Konikoff, David Eisner, Rabbi Myriam
Klotz, Rabbi Margot Stein, Marci Gilbert, and Rabbi Shalom
Schachter; Jason Shulman and Rabbi Zalman Schachter-Shalomi,
for their comments and support over the years of writing this book.

Special thanks to all the professional staff and lay leadership, past
and present, with whom I have worked over the years at the Jewish
Reconstructionist Federation: Lani Moss, Hattie Dunbar, Lawrence

Bush, Rabbi Shai Gluskin, Dan Cedarbaum, Rabbi Jeff Eisenstat, Rabbi Fredi Cooper, Mark Seal, Rabbi Moti Rieber, Rabbi Elisa Goldberg, Richard Haimowitz, Bob Barkin, Sandy Rubenstein, Devorah Servi, Dina April, Melanie Schneider, Jackie Land, and many other regional staff and lay leadership. Thanks as well to Joyce Norden, Dr. David Teutsch, director of the Reconstructionist Rabbinical College's "Ethics Center," and Rabbi Richard Hirsh, executive director of the Reconstructionist Rabbinical Association, for providing additional resources and support.

Shira Stutman worked diligently and creatively with me at the Jewish Reconstructionist Federation to produce a leadership curriculum of money and Jewish values that works to deepen and integrate the learning in this area.

The dedicated members of the following communities across North America contributed to the research and development of this project: Rabbi Fred Dobb of Congregation Adat Shalom, Maryland; Rabbi Toba Spitzer, Wendy Gedanken, Gwen Offerdahl, Clifford Goldsmith, and Cliff Cohen of Congregation Dorshei Tzedek, Massachusetts; Congregation Mishkan Shalom, Pennsylvania; Howard Ellegant of the Jewish Reconstructionist Congregation, Illinois; and numerous other individuals, organizations, and faith communities from across North America.

Many others contributed time, wisdom, and resources at various stages of this project. My apologies go to anyone who has not been appropriately credited.

I thank You, the Source of All Life, for the opportunity to attempt to bring sacred consciousness into a realm where we actively experience Your presence in our actions, and strive for a world where holiness and wholeness manifests in our communal, work, and home lives.

Rabbi Shawn Israel Zevit
Philadelphia, 2005/5765

OFFERINGS OF THE HEART

1

THE JEWISH WAY

Text, Tradition, and Today

The Talmud teaches, "One who wishes to acquire wisdom
should study the ways of the society (money), for there
is no greater area of Torah-study than this.
It is like an ever-flowing stream."
—Babylonian Talmud, *Bava Batra* 175b

From making decisions about marketing and publicity to budgeting
and setting dues schedules, our policies and choices reflect our individual commitments and the collective covenant of our community.
Each congregation expresses its own particular set of values and principles in its decision making around money. Each congregation is
also part of a larger network of communities within its own religious
stream. Even if it is identified as "unaffiliated" or "independent,"
no organization or congregation operates in a "values-free zone."
As the text above suggests, the ever-flowing stream of communal
life gives us a rich stage on which to demonstrate and examine the
values we hold, and the Torah, literally "the teaching," we embrace.

We are all influenced by the religious and cultural legacies, and
personal histories, that have given birth to the very unique communal expression of our faith traditions, and we are all part of the larger
society that carries norms and values around money. Studying and
reflecting on sacred texts has been seen as a compelled and compelling spiritual practice or "mitzvah" for the Jewish people for centuries. It has also been one of the main ways religious thought and
practice have been conveyed.

This section follows a model of studying Jewish sources from the perspective of Judaism as an unfolding religious civilization. Included are texts from biblical times to the present, compiled in order to deepen our understanding of a given issue.

Included for study and reflection are textual sources from the Bible, Mishnah, Talmud, Midrash, as well as medieval and contemporary writings on financial resources. As the texts are presented and discussed, think creatively about ways that you can bring these texts back to your community and use them as teaching tools. You may want to consider using these texts in the following ways:

- As the subject of a *Dvar Torah* or sermon
- As a topic for a newsletter article
- As a topic for an adult education class
- As prayerful intention-setting for a board, budget, or finance committee meeting
- As a study or prayer moment for a fundraising visit or launching a fundraising initiative
- As a *kavannah* (intention-setting) for a new building or sanctuary
- As a text for your mission statement, bylaws, or communal guidelines
- As part of your youth and adult education
- As part of a decision-making process on allocating charitable gifts
- As an opening for a *shabbaton* or communal retreat
- As an exploration of the ways values are suggested by different texts
- As an inquiry into how traditions and values from a different era are or are not relevant today and, if not, how they might be restated
- As an exploration of experiences in your community that relate to one of these texts
- As a starting point for any number of creative approaches to understanding the past and examining the present

Thus, when you engage a sacred text from the past, or a document that expresses your communal mission or current financial policies, you are both unlocking the essence of what has been distilled and preserved in it, and opening up to the values and beliefs you hold today, individually and communally.

The Hebrew Bible and the
Birth of Jewish Peoplehood

To illustrate the approach to text study and exegesis I described in the introduction to this chapter, I have adapted a lesson from Rabbi Toba Spitzer's series on money and Jewish values, conducted at congregation Dorshei Tzedek in Newton, Massachussetts.[1] Using a format such as the one below, or one you create yourself, you can approach any of the following texts in an interactive fashion that teaches participants about their religious heritage and spiritual wisdom and elicits discussion about money in general or a particular financial issue.

An Introduction to Building the Mishkan

One way to understand the book of Exodus is to see it as the story of the creation of a free, holy community. The first thing the Israelites are asked to build, and to pay for, is the portable sanctuary in the desert, the *Mishkan*.[2] The Mishkan of the desert was known primarily as the precursor to the Temple in Jerusalem.

But let's look at the Mishkan on a symbolic level. An enormous amount of space in the Torah is devoted to the Mishkan, so clearly it is important. What, really, is the Mishkan? God tells Moses to have the people build the Mishkan so that God's presence might dwell "among them." Not in the "place," but among the people. Not a structure that God lives in, but a structure that facilitates God's being with the people. We can understand this not just as a physical structure, but as any communal structure that somehow enables God's presence to be among us. If we understand God as a power of love and justice, then the Mishkan is the type of community we need to realize that power.

Text Study

Look at these texts from the books of Exodus and Nehemiah with this assumption: they have something to teach us about the building of community, and even more specifically about the role of money and material resources in that task. There were apparently two methods of paying for the Mishkan, of getting the materials needed: read Exodus 30:11-16, Nehemiah 10:33 (an example from the start of the second Temple period), and Exodus 35:21-29. Note that in the

text from Exodus 35, the people end up bringing more than enough,
and Moses had to tell them to stop.

> And God spoke to Moses, saying: When you take the sum of the
> children of Israel, according to their number, each shall pay God
> an expiation for his soul on being counted, that no plague may come
> upon them in being counted. This is what everyone who is being
> entered in the records shall pay: a half-shekel by sanctuary weight . . .
> as an offering to God. Everyone who is entered in the records
> from the age of twenty years up shall give God's offering. The rich
> shall not pay more and the poor shall not pay less than the half-
> shekel when giving God's offering as an expiation for your souls.
> You shall take the expiation money from the Israelites and assign it
> to the service of the Tent of Meeting; it shall serve as a reminder
> before God, as expiation for your souls. (Exod. 30:11-16)

> We laid upon ourselves obligations; To charge ourselves one-
> third of a shekel yearly for the service of the House of our God.
> (Neh. 10:33)

> Everyone who excelled in ability and everyone whose spirit moved
> them came, bringing to the LORD their offering for the work of
> the Tent of Meeting and for all its service and for the sacral vest-
> ments. Men and women, all whose hearts moved them, all who
> would make an elevation offering of gold to the LORD, came bring-
> ing brooches, earrings, rings, and pendants—gold objects of all
> kinds. And everyone who had in his possession blue, purple, and
> crimson yarns, fine linen, goats' hair, tanned ram skins, and dol-
> phin skins, brought them; everyone who would make gifts of sil-
> ver or copper brought them as gifts for the LORD; and everyone
> who had in his possession acacia wood for any work of the service
> brought that. And all the skilled women spun with their own hands,
> and brought what they had spun, in blue, purple, and crimson
> yarns, and in fine linen. And all the women who excelled in that
> skill spun the goats' hair. And the chieftains brought lapis lazuli
> and other stones for setting, for the ephod and for the breastpiece;
> and spices and oil for lighting, for the anointing oil, and for the
> aromatic incense. Thus the Israelites, all the men and women
> whose hearts moved them to bring anything for the work that
> the LORD, through Moses, had commanded to be done, brought
> it as a freewill offering to the LORD. (Exod. 35:21-29)

HEVRUTAH

Invite participants to group into *hevrutah* (pairs) and read through the texts again. The goal with each text is to understand what values can be drawn from this text. Give a fixed time limit according to your situation, ask the *hevrutah* partners to read the texts out loud to each other, and make sure each person gets a chance to speak. Questions for Exodus 30:11-16 might include the following: "What is the spiritual power of each person 'being counted' through the bringing of the half-shekel?" "What is the relationship of this act to 'atonement'?" "Why do you think that God specifies that the rich and poor must each pay the same amount?" (Keep in mind that the half-shekel was a small amount, more of a token sum than a substantive fee.) For Exodus 35:21-29, why is the concept of "freewill offerings of the heart" introduced? Who is invited to give here that was not in the half-shekel text? How do you value different skills and offerings in your own community, besides financial gifts?

CLOSING DISCUSSION

Reconvene, and have participants share what they came up with. Record the essential values inherent in each insight on a chart. Are these values we think are important? Which seem most important to you? Afterwards, open up discussion. How could these teachings be useful in your community? What are you already doing? What might you do? What stands in the way of implementing some of these values? Summarize insights.

In a similar fashion, treat the rest of this chapter as a foundational resource for your own personal, congregational, or organizational exploration. In no way do the texts I have selected represent the totality of Jewish thought and practice in the realm of money and Jewish values. This is simply a beginning point that will hopefully inspire you to look at the wealth of Jewish material on this subject, or the richness of your own religious tradition. You could use any of the sources in this chapter and follow a process similar to the one outlined above.

What becomes apparent in the Hebrew Bible early in the exodus story and in God's partnership with Moses and the Israelites is that justice, and the pursuit of justice, underlies the relationship from the start. Compassionate action in regards to material goods and work is the focus of one of the first collection of laws governing the Jewish people.

> If you lend money to My people, to the poor among you, do not
> act towards them as a creditor, exact no interest from them. If you
> take your neighbor's garment in pledge, you must return it to him
> before the sun sets; it is his only clothing, the sole covering for his
> skin. In what else shall he sleep? Therefore, if he cries out to Me, I
> will pay heed, for I am a compassionate God. (Exod. 22:24-6)

It is not only God's inherent justice that is to be a benchmark for
ethical action in the realm of compensation, but the experience of
the Jewish people themselves, having been enslaved and oppressed,
that is to serve as a constant reminder where the execution of justice
and the use of money may overlap, as seen in the following quota-
tion from Exodus:

> You shall not subvert the rights of your needy in disputes. Keep far
> from a false charge; do not bring death on those who are innocent
> and in the right, for I will not acquit the wrongdoer. Do not take
> bribes, for bribes blind the clear-sighted and upset the pleas of
> those who are in the right. You shall not oppress the stranger for
> you know the feelings of the stranger, having yourselves been
> strangers in Egypt. (Exod. 23:6-9)

> You shall not falsify measures of length, weight, or capacity. You
> shall have an honest balance, honest weights, and honest "ephah"
> and an honest "hin" [measures of grain]. I the Lord am your God
> who freed you from the land of Egypt. You shall faithfully observe
> all My laws and My rules; I am God. (Lev. 19:35-37)

The warning against using material resources to pervert justice finds
its most poetic expression in these lines from Deuteronomy:

> You shall not judge unfairly: you shall show no partiality; you shall
> take no bribes, for bribes blind the eyes of the discerning and up-
> set the pleas of the just. "Tzedek, tzedek tirdof" [Justice, justice
> shall you pursue]. (Deut. 16:18-20)

The dispensation of justice, support of the communal religious center and the priesthood, and offerings of one's heart according to
means were not the only ways to ensure that economic resources
and their uses reflected God's plan for Israelite society. Those who

were blessed with land, a harvest and produce, were asked to provide for those who did not share this abundance and remember their roots of impoverishment:

> When you reap the harvest in the field and overlook a sheaf in the field, do not turn back to get it; it shall go to the stranger, the fatherless, and the widow, in order that the Lord your God may bless you in all your undertakings. When you beat down the fruit of your olive trees, do not go over them again; they shall go to the stranger, the fatherless, and the widow. When you gather the grapes of your vineyard, do not pick it over again; that shall go to the stranger, the fatherless, and the widow. Always remember that you were a slave in the land of Egypt, therefore do I enjoin you to observe this commandment. (Deut. 24:19-22)

At the same time the Divine source and ownership of wealth was core to the emerging understanding of the basis of wealth in Israelite society. One was obligated to give both a tenth of one's produce to sacred service, those in need, and also to use their produce to celebrate the very abundance and sustaining of life regardless of the total sum yield. Multiple avenues of giving and resource allocation are already present in biblical times: looking after oneself and one's family, one's community, one's central holy institutions and those who served in them.

> You shall set aside every year a tenth part of all the yield of your sowing that is brought from the field. You shall consume the tithes of your new grain and wine and oil, and the firstlings of your herd and flocks, in the presence of the Lord your God... But do not neglect the Levite in your community, for he has no hereditary portion as you have. Every third year you shall bring out a full tithe of your yield that year, but leave it within your settlements. Then the Levite... and the fatherless, and the widow in your settlements shall come and eat at their fill, so that the Lord your God may bless you in all the enterprises you undertake. (Deut. 14:22-23, 27-29)

In fact, in a rare occurrence in the Bible, an actual speech is scripted for the owner of the land to say upon fulfilling the requirement of tithing:

> When you have set aside the full tenth part of your yield—in the third year of the tithe—and have given it to the Levite, the stranger, the fatherless, and the widow, that they may eat their fill in your settlements, you shall declare before the Lord your God: "I have cleared out the consecrated portion from the house; and I have given it to the Levite, the stranger, the fatherless, and the widow, just as You have commanded me; I have neither transgressed nor neglected any of Your commandments ....I have obeyed the Lord my God; I have done just as You have commanded me. Look down from Your holy abode, from heaven, and bless Your people Israel and the soil You have given us, a land flowing with milk and honey, as You swore to our ancestors." (Deut. 26:12-15)

After the establishment of the Israelite kingdoms, the prophets become the main voice for a God-centered life based on justice and compassion. Reading any of the prophets for their sense of equity in communal relations is worthwhile and inspiring. For our purposes I am citing two of Isaiah's declarations as it pertains to money and social justice. A rich perspective on life and a reliance on God as opposed to the human monetary system alone are seen as key to a satisfied life:

> Ho, all those who are thirsty, come for water,
> Even if you have no money, come, buy food and eat . . .
> Why do you spend money for what is not bread,
> Your earnings for what does not satisfy?
> . . . Incline your ear and come to Me;
> Hearken and you shall be revived. (Isa. 55:1-3)

Later, Isaiah challenges the split between business in the world and the business of a God-centered life. In one of his passages, made widely known by its inclusion in the Yom Kippur service, a day of repentance, fasting, and prayer, he states:

> "Why, when we fasted, did You not see?
> When we starved our bodies, did You pay no heed?"
> Because on your fast day you see to your business
> And oppress your laborers!
> . . . Is such the fast I desire
> A day for men to starve their bodies?
> . . . No, this is the fast that I desire:

To unlock the fetters of wickedness,
And untie the cords of lawlessness
To let the oppressed go free;
To break off every yoke.
To share your bread with the hungry,
And to take the wretched into your home;
When you see the naked to clothe him,
And not to ignore your own kin. (Isa. 58:3-7)

The later books in the Hebrew Bible or *Tanach* come out of what is called the wisdom tradition. Here, the Torah, God's teaching and presence, is depicted as the very embodiment of wisdom in our lives, and the attainment of wisdom and the integration of it into daily action as a path to living in the Divine image:

Happy is the person who finds wisdom, the person who attains understanding.
Her value in trade is better than silver, her yield is greater than gold.
She is more precious than rubies: all of your goods cannot equal her.
In her right hand is length of days, in her left, riches and honor.
Her ways are pleasant ways, and all her paths, peaceful.
She is a tree of life to those who grasp her, and whoever holds on to her is happy. (Prov. 3:13-18)

Wealth and generosity may be experienced in the form of material resources for most people, but the writer also points out that the act of giving tied to doing what is right is often a spiritual barometer of whether one is able to truly appreciate what one has in life:

One person gives generously and ends with more
Another stints on doing the right thing and incurs a loss (Prov. 11:24-25).

As we have seen in this brief overview of biblical texts, money and material resources are depicted as emanating from God, and the use of those resources in just, compassionate, wise, and sustainable ways is understood as an ultimate human responsibility to God and community. As well, numerous methods of striking a balance between the "haves and have-nots" were woven into the fabric of Israelite society. Wealth and the creation of wealth were not seen as sinful or against God's will as long as the use and method of obtaining these resources were not exploitative. There was no glorification of poverty and holding private property was seen as normative.

These ideals were an ongoing challenge to uphold, as we see in the prophets and later biblical books. At times, internal and external strife or prosperity led to an abandonment of these core Jewish principals by segments of leadership and ancient Israelite society. Nonetheless, the view of the Divine ownership of wealth and our role as managers of the resources in our midst was the foundation for the rabbinic laws and ethical treatises that followed.

THE SAGES SPEAK

The rabbinic sages, whose teachings from about 200 BCE to 200 CE were compiled by Rabbi Yehudah Hanasi in the *Mishnah* (the teaching), dealt with the emerging realities of living as a Jew in a post-biblical world under the Greeks and later the Romans. The destruction of the Second Temple by the Roman army in 70 CE, and the Jews' later failure to unseat the Roman occupation in the Bar Kochba revolt of 135 CE, left the remaining rabbis and other communal leaders navigating a challenging and increasingly hostile terrain of religious, socio-political, and economic life. Building on biblical tradition and responding to changing needs, the rabbis developed the tradition of *Vi'asu seyag L'Torah* (building a fence around the Torah).[3]

As Leonard Kravitz and Kerry Olitzky state in their commentary on *Pirke Avot* (The Ethics of the Sages), "The rabbis used the metaphor of a fence around the Torah as a means of protecting the essence of Torah in the midst of a proliferation of new demands. The insights into the Law that they had already developed would need protection, even as they knew the Torah would need to grow if the Jewish community was to survive."[4]

Later rabbinic sources qualified this idea by pointing out that, while a fence is important, it should never be more important than what it fences in. As if to parallel the idea of Jewish law being a good boundary marker and semi-permeable layer of protection for biblical teaching, the value and importance of contributing part of one's financial resources or produce to those who did not have and equalizing wealth, is expressed in the following: "Tithes are a fence around wealth" (Mishnah *Avot* 3:13).

The rabbis also connected an understanding of serving God with all one's being to the primary declaration of faith in the Hebrew Bible, the *Shema* ("Listen, O Israel, the Lord is our God, God is

One," Deut. 6:4-5). The following example from the Mishnah is both profound in spiritual insight, and foundational to the rabbinic concept that human beings are stewards of Divine blessings, especially in the areas of money and material possessions:

> Listen! Israel, the Source of Life is our God, God alone! And you must love the One your God with all your heart, and with all your soul, and with all your abundance. (Deut. 6:4-5)

> "With all your heart" means with both positive and negative inclinations (the heart is the seat of wisdom—mindfulness and consciousness). "With all your soul" means though your life eventually goes back to God. "With all your abundance" means with all your wealth. (material and spiritual).[5]

The primary declaration of God's unity in a diverse world is intimately tied to how faith in the One is expressed in every facet of life. Wealth, not only in terms of quantity but the use of whatever resources one has, is connected to the Divine Source. In fact, in a discussion about what constitutes wealth, which ranges from having a loving and respected spouse to having a bathroom near your dining area, Ben Zoma declares: "Who is rich? The person who rejoices in their portion . . ." (Mishnah *Avot* 4:1).

The rabbis developed hundreds of laws and ethical sayings about work, money, and possessions. Their commentary on the Mishnah, known as the *Gemarah,* was later compiled in two versions, one from ancient Palestine and the other from Babylonia, to form the Talmud. Here they continued to emphasize the idea of the Divine source of wealth: "Our Rabbis taught: Who is wealthy? The one who has pleasure of soul in their wealth: this is Rabbi Meir's view" (Babylonian Talmud, *Shabbat* 25b).

> Rabbi Meir said: One should always teach their child a clean and easy craft, and earnestly pray to the One to Whom all wealth and property belong, for neither property nor wealth comes from one's calling, but from the One to whom wealth and property belong, as it is said, "The silver is mine, and the gold is mine, says the Lord of Hosts." (Babylonian Talmud, *Kiddushin* 82b)

There is another wonderful Talmudic story about balancing spiritual pursuit, religious practice, and tending to material needs. While the teaching has a fantastical element to it, knowing the rabbis were predominantly tradespeople who spent a portion of the day in their carpentry or blacksmith shops adds a practical dimension to Rabbi Yishmael's gleaning:

> For a period of time a Roman decree did not allow the study of Torah. Rabbi Shimon bar Yochai hid away to keep studying, spending many years in a cave buried up to his neck, with only a carob tree for sustenance. When he finally came out he saw a man working in a field. He thought to himself, "there is so little time to study God's word and you devote yourself to insignificant things like settlement of the world." His spirit had become so purified during the time in seclusion that his angry gaze was enough to turn the farmer into dust. Farther down the road, seeing other laborers the scene repeated itself. A Heavenly Voice called out, "unless you refrain from turning my world into chaos, I will put you back into your cave!" Rabbi Yishmael derives the following teaching from this: spiritual study is needed, but the Divine plan makes it necessary to devote time to providing for one's own material needs. (Babylonian Talmud, *Berachot* 35b)

The Talmud contains discussions about the alleviation of poverty and the rights of those who are underprivileged, but there are no ascetic vows to remove oneself from community. Mass accumulation or striving for wealth was seen as destroying spiritual priorities. The Divine ownership of wealth is central to the principles of traditional Jewish economic philosophy at the personal, communal, national, and universal levels. First fruits are given to the Temple, thanking God for bountiful produce. The land is in the hands of the Divine and must rest every seven years and lie fallow. Our entire material world is on loan, and all goods must be returned to their original owners every fiftieth year for the Jubilee. Material and spiritual freedom are intimately linked, and the basis of all is not financial equity, but the pursuit of justice.[6]

In their book, *Tough Choices,* Albert Vorspan and David Saperstein outline a couple of the methods the sages established for distributing funds to those in need in the community.

> From the second century [CE] . . . every Jewish community had two basic funds. The first was called the *kuppah* [box] and served the local poor only. The indigent were given funds to supply their needs for an entire week. The second fund was called *tamchui*

[bowl] and consisted of a daily distribution of food to both itiner-
ants and residents. The funds' administrators, selected from among
the leaders of the community, were expected to be persons of highest integrity. The *kuppah* was administered by three trustees who
acted as a *beit din* [court]. They determined the merit of appli-
cants and the amounts to be given. The fund was always operated
under the strictest regulations. To avoid suspicion, collections were
always made by at least two persons. They were authorized to tax
all members of the community, including *tzedakah* recipients according to their capacity to pay, testimony to the principal that no
individual was free from responsibility for the welfare of all. If necessary, they seized property until the amount was paid."[7]

Even through the centuries following the destruction of the Second
Temple and the cessation of many Temple-related practices, the rabbis continued to draw inspiration and create new guidelines to religious practice based on the biblical principles. The teachings and
practices they developed and their adherence to *halakhik* standards
served as boundaries to excessive behavior, especially around wealth
and material resources. This included the obligation to take care of
the poor and those in need.

THE MEDIEVAL PERIOD

Over many centuries Jewish communities sprang up around Europe,
initially from the Middle East under the Christian Roman Empire,
and then later under the rule of the Moslem Empire. Jewish laws
and teaching around money followed Jews wherever they settled,
reflecting the Jewish leadership's attempt to strike a balance between
the resources needed for Jewish families and communities and those
needed to pay the rulers of the countries in which they lived. In
most of Europe, Jews were not allowed to own land and lived at the
pleasure of the governing body. Saperstein and Vorspan describe
this period the following way:

By the Middles Ages, community responsibility encompassed every aspect of life. The Jewish community regulated market prices
so that the poor could purchase food and other basic commodities
at cost. Wayfarers were issued tickets, good for meals and lodging
at homes of members of the community, who took turns in offering hospitality. Both these practices anticipated 'meal tickets' and

modern food stamp plans. Some Jewish communities even established 'rent control,' directing that the poor be given housing at
rates they could afford. In Lithuania, local trade barriers were re-
laxed for poor refugees. When poor young immigrants came from
other places, the community would support them until they com-
pleted their education or earned a trade.

The organization of tzedakah became so specialized that numerous societies were established to keep pace with all the needs.
Each of the following functions was assumed by a different society
on behalf of the community at large: visiting the sick, burying the
dead, furnishing dowries for poor girls, providing clothing, ran-
soming captives, supplying maternity needs, and providing necessities for observing holidays. In addition there were public inns for
travelers, homes for the aged, orphanages, and free medical care.
As early as the eleventh century, a *hekdesh* [hospital] was established by the Jewish community of Cologne, primarily for poor
and sick travelers. Many medieval Jewish communities in Poland
and Germany adopted this pattern.[8]

While Biblical and Rabbinic law continued to be at the center of
religious practice, the new and expanded definitions of what it meant
to be a responsible member of a community developed to meet changing circumstances. Moslem Spain provided a fertile and relatively
safe ground for the development of Jewish thought. In this text,
Maimonides (Spain, 1135–1204) outlines the responsibilities and
benefits of being a new member of a community:

> One who settles in a community for thirty days becomes obligated
> to contribute to the charity fund together with the other members
> of the community. One who settles there for three months be-
> comes obligated to contribute clothing with which the poor of
> the community can cover themselves. One who settles there for
> nine months becomes obligated to contribute to the burial fund
> for burying the community's poor and providing for all of their
> needs of burial. (Maimonides, Mishneh Torah, Gifts to the Poor,
> 9:12)

Notice the parallel of being born as a full member of a religious
community to the natural cycle of human development and birth.
Also, the acknowledgement of steps along the way to full membership can relate to our contemporary discussions of membership and
dues. A time-delayed gift-giving period, a progressive movement in

the *halakhik* system of holy tasks, and some definition for what the community's responsibility is to the individual financial or material resources are also provided. Continuing the rabbinic tradition, Maimonides reminds the Jewish community of their financial responsibilities towards each other as well as their responsibility to grow spiritually: "One should not aim first at accumulating wealth and then devoting time to the study of Torah . . . but sacred study that is not accompanied by economic activity is liable to end in sin and robbing others" (Maimonides, Mishneh Torah, Hilchot Talmud Torah, 3:7, 10).

Maimonides advocated pursuing "the middle way," as had many sages throughout the ages. His ideal life mix was one-third Torah study, one-third livelihood, and one-third attending to physical needs and general interests.

Yehuda Halevi, another medieval poet and philosopher also picked up on this economic-religious integration when he discusses piety and wealth:

> Decreasing one's wealth is not an act of piety if such wealth happens to have been gained in a lawful way and its further acquisition does not prevent a person from occupying himself with Torah and righteous deeds, especially for one who has family and dependants and whose desire is to spend his money for the sake of God....For you are, as it were, enjoying God's hospitality, being invited to God's table, and should thank God for God's bounty, both inwardly and outwardly. (Yehuda Halevi, Kuzari 11:50)

Bachya Ibn Pakuda, an eleventh-century Jewish philosopher and judge, who lived in Moslem Spain, wrote about money and serving God as a means for doing sacred action in the world:

> One who trusts God is not hampered in his trust by great wealth because he does not rely on it. He sees it as a reserve he has been commanded to make use of under certain specific and temporary circumstances. He does not become arrogant if he remains wealthy, he never reminds anyone he gave money to what he did for him and he never asks compliments for his gratitude. Instead he thanks his Creator for having made him an agent of His kindness. (Bachya Ibn Pakuda, Duties of the Heart, Introduction to the Fourth Gate)[9]

Ibn Pakuda, in his book *Duties of the Heart,* goes on at length to counsel an arms-length relationship with financial resources, trying

to inculcate a perspective that would connect humanity to God regardless of means, and see money as a God-given gift that supports
the individual, their dependents, the community, as well as future
generations.

In the late twelfth century, a Jewish pietist movement developed
in Germany, known as *Chasidei Ashkenaz* ("the pious ones of
Ashkenaz"—the area of Europe that would give rise to the term
"Ashkenazi Jews"). Yehudah HeChasid, in his ethical work *Sefer
Chasidim* (The Book of the Pious), documents the almost severe
adherence to religious practice and the deep longing for spiritual
purity that the Chasidei Ashkenaz followed. There is a whole chapter on *tzedakah* in which a number of emerging issues about money,
communal life, and human behavior are discussed:

> Only a person who is as trustworthy as Rabbi Chaninah ben
> Teradyon is qualified for the post of administrator of a communal
> charity fund.[10]
>
> But a . . . person who is forgetful should not be nominated as
> administrator, no matter how upright and moral he may be, for he
> will forget how much he paid out, and he cannot be trusted to
> receive donations for it may slip his mind.[11] (Yehudah HeChasid,
> Sefer Chasidim, 192 [329])

The ethical characteristics of the person entrusted with giving
tzedakah in the community, even if they are well intentioned and
pious, are weighed against the skills needed to ensure that monies
make it to their intended source. This practical check and balance as
part of religious practice develops along with the growth and increasing complexity of human society. Yehuda continues to explore
these themes as he writes about the ethics of being a treasurer:

> You cannot satisfy everybody. Sometimes a treasurer of a charity
> fund gives money to dignified people who are in straitened cir-
> cumstances. He should tell only two or three of the leading mem-
> bers of the community, because if the matter became public
> knowledge it would be a source of deep embarrassment to the
> recipient....The treasurer should not pay attention to vile charac-
> ters who say they don't trust him. But if the majority of the commu-
> nity expresses displeasure and wants to depose him, he should say to
> the board of directors, "Since the majority of the members are op-
> posed to me, go ahead and elect someone who is to your liking."[12]

A Touch of Mysticism in the Everyday

The *Kabbalah* (the Jewish mystical tradition that went through a profound stage of development in Jewish thought and practice in the thirteenth to sixteenth centuries in Europe and the Middle East) explores the idea that reality exists on four levels or "worlds" simultaneously: the worlds of *assiyah* or "action" (physical), *yetzirah* or "formation" (emotional), *beriyah* or "creation" (intellectual), and *atzilut* or "emanation" (spiritual). Each four of these worlds are seen as existing within each of the four, a world of circles within circles of God's manifestation in the world. As financial matters were not separated from spiritual pursuits, the *kabbalistic* reality map saw money and material goods as existing in each of these four worlds as well.

In Rabbi Nitlon Bonder's *The Kabbalah of Money*,[13] he builds on classical *kabbalah*, adding his own perspective on livelihood. In the world of action, he suggests we see the material world manifesting as livelihood, as material goods and gain. In the world of formation, the level of perception is elusive, with the reality of means being experienced on an emotional level, as something we treasure for reasons beyond material comfort and sustenance. In the world of creation, material resources take on a symbolic presence in our minds, and manifest in livelihood on the basis of merit. Finally, in the world of emanation, inner perception is hidden from us, and in reality there is a connection to the infinite that is impossible to articulate as gain in any way.

It is possible for us to look at any financial matter from these four perspectives and ask: what is the consequence of a given financial transaction on the physical, emotional, intellectual and spiritual well-being of the individuals and communities with whom I share the transaction? From the Jewish mystical perspective this would be looking at the totality of God's manifestation in any given action, and a way of bringing more holiness into everyday reality as what is sometimes termed "normative mysticism." The ultimate goal is both *tikkun hanefesh* (repairing the soul) and *tikkun olam* (repairing the world). Thus each material transaction holds the potential of enlivening ourselves and our world in the pursuit of a livelihood. Rabbi Bonder goes on to say:

> The rabbis developed the concept of "yishuv olam," the effort to
> settle the world. Derived from Genesis 2:15, where human beings

are assigned the task "to till and tend" the land, this concept states that we should constantly try, while maintaining an honest relationship with the world, to increase the overall quality of life. It is the duty of every one of us to expand wealth—and not only our own—into the world around us. Let us define wealth as the highest level of organization possible to the environment in such a way that everything alive and everything essential to life exists without scarcity. In other words, the more abundance we create for a given human need, without generating the scarcity of another need, the better. This is every person's duty: to improve the quality of life around him or her.[14]

MODERN MUSINGS

As nation states emerged, and the industrial revolution gave rise to more complex societies, Jews have continued to respond to the new challenges by using Jewish tradition and teaching as a base from which to respond to changing circumstance. Moshe Chayim Luzzato, in a widely studied text from his early-eighteenth-century moralistic work *Mesilat Yesharim,* states:

> Most people are not outright thieves, taking their neighbors' property and putting it in their own premises. However, in their business dealing most of them get a taste of stealing whenever they permit themselves to make an unfair profit at the expense of someone else, claiming that such a profit has nothing to do with stealing. It is not merely the obvious and explicit theft with which we have to concern ourselves, but any unlawful transfer of wealth from one individual to another that may occur in everyday economic activities.[15]

At the dawn of the seventeenth century, Jewish spiritual renewal exploded in Eastern Europe, building on the Jewish mystical tradition of the *kabbalah* and adding a more populist approach to connecting with God, Jewish tradition, and practice. Charismatic *rebbes* arose and with them many followers who were looking for a more emotive and spontaneous expression of Jewish religious life. The Baal Shem Tov was the first master of modern Hasidism, and while he did not write himself, his teachings were compiled by his disciples, and his influence is found in those who came after him as demonstrated in this story of economics and spiritual life:

Rabbi Nachman Kossover, a disciple of the Baal Shem Tov, was speaking to some Hasidim who he saw were failing to fulfill "I have placed God before me always" when they were engaged in their livelihood, in commerce, and business dealings. They asked him how it was possible to think of God at that time. He answered that just as they were well able to think of their business dealings while they were supposed to be praying, so could they fulfill "I have placed God before me always" when they were engaged in business.[16]

Using the story of the Israelites' forty-year journey in the wilderness as a metaphor for a simpler time than the modern world and its challenges to seeing money as a spiritual tool, a hasidic teacher, Schmuel of Sochochow, Poland, early twentieth century, writes:

They lacked a confidence in their spiritual ability to handle the everyday challenges of earning an economic existence in a normal way. As long as they lived in the desert, God provided them daily with Manna from heaven. Their water came from the miraculous spring of Miriam, and they were sheltered from the blazing sun by the Divine Clouds of Glory....Wealth was no spiritual challenge for them. However, going into the Land of Israel, where their livelihood would have to be earned through the normal processes of agriculture, industry and trade, meant that they would be faced with the challenge of economic morality. They feared their own ability to meet that challenge. They preferred the sanctity of the Divine provider in the desert to the danger of the challenge of wealth and it was this that caused them to bring back false reports that would keep them in the desert.[17]

With greater demands on time and more complex economic systems developing, the need for some distinction between everyday financial demands and time for spiritual revitalization and reflection has also intensified. Rav Kook, the first chief rabbi of Israel until his death in 1935 put it the following way:

The individual recovers from the influence of the material and the mundane at regular intervals every Shabbat day. What the Shabbat achieves for the individual the Jubilee year achieves for the society as a whole. This temporary suspension of normal economic routine raises the Nation spiritually and morally.[18]

PRAYER ON LITURGY AND LIVELIHOOD

In the first two millennia of the Jewish people's journey, the tempo-rary sanctuary, and later the two Temples, provided a focus for the individual and communal expression to God. Offerings of grain or sacrificing of animals was a way to show thanks for abundance or an attempt to ensure it in ancient times. With the fall of the Second Temple in 70 CE, prayer and liturgy became, as the sages termed it, the service of the heart, replacing the sacrificial cult. Ba-sic human hopes and concerns did not disappear with the end of the Second Commonwealth in Israel, and the liturgy that evolved around that time and since has encompassed economic needs as part of spiritual conversation and public worship. In the *Shmoneh Esreh* (Amidah), the great standing prayer or nineteen blessings (week-day), said both silently or aloud at all prayer services, there is one blessing for abundance:

> Grant blessing over us, Abundant One,
> upon this year, and all its forms of produce;
> let it be a year of good.
> and give blessing on the earth,
> and satisfy us with your goodness,
> and give blessing to this year,
> as in the good years of the past.
> Blessed are You, All Bountiful,
> who gives blessing to the years.[19]

The above prayer can be seen as a request for God's intervention in the world to provide abundance, and it can also be seen as a way of cultivating a perspective of abundance in life and the ap-preciation for all the blessings from the One "who gives blessing to the years."

There is also an optional prayer for sustenance and well-being that can be said as part of the sixteenth blessing of the Amidah, the prayer for the hopeful acceptance of our prayers themselves:

> You are The Provider, God who feeds, supports and sustains all
> creatures, from the mighty horned oxen to the tiny new-hatched
> nestlings. May You grant me proper sustenance, supply to me and
> to my household nourishment, forestalling any state of need. Pro-
> vide in pleasure, not in pain, in willingness, not in begrudging, in
> honor, not in shame, for life and well-being, from the flow of

prosperity, from the blessing from above, so that I may better do Your will, and occupy myself with Your Torah and uphold Your *mitzvot*. Give me freedom from dependence upon others, that this verse of Scripture might apply to me, as well: "Providing with an open hand, you satisfy the wishes of all life" (Psalm 145:16). And also what is written: "Cast yourself upon the Bountiful, and God will be your sustenance" (Psalm 55:23).[20]

Interestingly, these prayers are two of thirteen petitionary prayers in the Amidah that is found in all the weekday services, but are omitted on Shabbat as part of the spiritual practice of letting go of personal requests to rest solely and soulfully in the place of praise and abundant Divine blessing. In that way Shabbat itself becomes a balancing energy to seeing money as a means to ensuring a livelihood and proposes God-centered living as a means to ensuring a healthy spiritual perspective.

In the fourth blessing of the grace after meals, the prayer appreciating "God's goodness," the themes of abundance (both the gratefulness and request for) appear as well: "God is, was, and will forever be bountiful with us, with grace and with kindness and with mercy, with relief, salvation, success, blessing, help, consolation, sustenance, support, mercy, life, and all good; and of all good things may God never deprive us."[21]

After the Torah is read on Shabbat, a series of prayers can be said that include a prayer for the congregation. Here the commitment to religious community through the offering of human and financial resources is appreciated at a moment when the largest number of people are usually assembled, and the central biblical teaching and discussion has taken place:

> May the One who blessed our ancestors, bless this entire holy community, along with other holy communities—them, their sons and daughters, and all that belongs to them. All those who set apart houses of assembly for prayer, and those who come into their midst to pray, and those who study Torah for the sake of teaching it to young and old, and those who provide light for lamps, and wine . . . and food for guests, and donations to the poor, and all those who are faithfully occupied with the needs of the community . . . may the blessed Holy One provide them their reward, and turn away from them every sickness, and heal their bodies, and pardon their failures. May God send blessing and success in all their efforts.[22]

℀

It would take an entire book in and of itself to explore the teachings and writings of modern Jewish writers as the Jewish community began to arrive and develop in North America and integrate into the modern nation-states. Some of these writings are woven throughout this book. Others can be found in more detail by looking at the bibliography and further resources.

The challenge of living as a citizen of a larger culture and remaining a member of the Jewish community are polarities that have at times been a source of creative tension for individual Jews, their households (representing a diversity of singles, couples with and without children, interfaith, gay, lesbian, observant and assimilated, and so on), congregations, and organizations in the Jewish community. At other times, the challenges of an open society with greater opportunity, affluence, and less systemic anti-Semitism have led to a polarization between Jewish religious practice and Jewish values and the practices and values of North American society that would inform choices and behavior around money and nurturing sacred community.

Rabbi Jamie Arnold reflected on the challenge of community, money, and faith by exploring a variety of approaches available to giving in community from a Jewish perspective. This particular article was written in response to increase in gift giving on the Jewish holiday of Hannukah, mirroring gift giving at Christmas. Not originally a Hannukah practice until the influence of North American culture, the opportunity and challenge in balancing emerging customs with Jewish tradition is ongoing.

> In every generation, Jewish communities, while striving to maintain our distinctive character, have adopted and adapted values, institutions, melodies, and customs from the cultures of neighboring peoples. . . . Mordecai Kaplan insisted that the incorporation of "contemporary" ideas and customs into our Jewish lives did not constitute a break with tradition. . . . We must, however, be wary of the folly of believing that such thoughtful integration is any easier than outright rejection or denial. . . . The challenge becomes: how does one selectively draw from the positive values of giving and yet avoid the pitfalls of excessive consumerism and materialism.[23]

Using a variety of Jewish sources, Rabbi Arnold goes on to suggest that in responding to the challenge we need to expand our notions of what constitutes a gift, or a contribution, to include the *gifts of joy*, "Better is one who shows a smiling countenance than one who offers milk to drink" (Babylonian Talmud, *Ketubot* 111b); the *gifts of words of kindness*, "whoever gives a small coin to a poor man has six blessings bestowed upon him, but the one who speaks a kind word to him obtains eleven blessings" (Babylonian Talmud, *Bava Batra* 9b); the *gifts of for-give-ness*, as described in the Bible through the various forgiveness offerings, the Jewish liturgy of the High Holy Days in particular, and the personal ability to give the gift of forgiveness to each other; the *gift of time*—contrary to the adage "time is money," Jewish religious tradition sees time as priceless—a full day like Shabbat, set aside to "spend" in prayer, with community, family, and friends creates, as Rabbi Abraham Joshua Heschel, a twentieth-century rabbi, thinker, and teacher would say, "a palace in time";[24] and the *gift of giving*, the opportunity to give material resources simply because we can and we desire to be generous.

Rabbi Arnold concludes with the following:

> At first glance it seems counterintuitive from an economic point of view to give when the flasks are few and the nights grow colder. But the scarcity reminds us of our interdependence, our need to rely on and support one another. And when we can take the leap of faith to share our limited resources we allow Divine light to shine through our humanity.[25]

Rabbis, lay leaders, teachers, and thinkers continue to wrestle with the issues of money and Jewish values and practice in all contemporary denominations of the Jewish people. Congregations continue to be at the nexus of these discussions. Those of us who are involved in building communities of faith are thus able to join the inquiry of the generations, even as we navigate the challenges and possibilities of developing values-based approaches in our congregations or organizations today.

The goal of this chapter has been to provide you with a sampling of Jewish sources that you can study, discuss, and look for application and relevance in the financial practices of your own community. You can also review your own mission statement, newsletter, brochure, programming, and educational offerings, and compare them with your budgets, revenues, and expenditures, examining them as texts that reveal your communal spiritual journey and stated values. I do not mean to imply that a faith community exploring its religious values automatically produces agreement. Agreeing as to which religious values are priorities can provoke intense and, at times, divisive debate. Even with a majority of values being shared, a community also needs to frame its perspective and actions through the lens of its individual and collective beliefs, attitudes, norms, claims and obligations, and so forth. Notwithstanding the need to avoid a triumphalist attitude about a values-based approach to money, the blend of traditional and contemporary wisdom can help us clarify our terms, examine our preexisting attitudes, and determine which among all our values and principles will guide us in the conscious and ethical management of our financial resources.

2

LIVING THE VISION

Mission and Values

For lack of vision a people lose direction.
—Prov. 29:18

Throughout the history of the Jewish people, the Torah, the Talmud (collections of rabbinic laws, discussions, stories, and ethical sayings), the *halakhik* (Jewish legal) codes, and the laws and customs of the countries in which Jews lived, served as guides for regulating interpersonal and communal relations. These traditions also gave members of a community their shared purpose, beliefs, and behaviors. In North American society, with greater focus on individual choice and voluntary participation in a religious community, there is both a practical (for example, bylaws and incorporation) and deeper spiritual need for self-definition in terms of the mission and values the community stands for. Outside of most orthodox communities, there is a wider range of personal religious practices, as well as definition and expression of what constitutes Jewish identity.

While sacred texts and traditions still inform our life, they do not by definition determine individual practice and beliefs for the vast majority of North American Jews. Even when *halakhah* guides our practice in the use of money, there can be clashes with other values and norms within our larger culture. How then do we convey what we stand for and what informs our very reason for coming together in voluntary faith communities?

The process of developing congregational or organizational mission statements, statements of principles, bylaws, and written policies, influences how we build and manage our communal life. The way financial resources are viewed, raised, and spent is intimately tied to who we say we are, and what we do to express our reason for being as a group.

In our faith communities, we may not have gone through a community-wide process to develop a shared mission, outside of drafting bylaws and legally incorporating, but there are reasons we have chosen to gather as a religious congregation in a time when other options for connection exist in our society. We may not have strategically planned for how we will achieve the dream that has drawn us together, yet our choices in programming and spending are contributing to how we develop now, and what kind of community we will become. We may not have a developed set of policies in our congregations, or we may have developed some agreed-upon standards in particular areas and not in others, yet our ritual practices, choices of worship styles and melodies, adult education, committee processes, and board structures all convey who we are.

The truth is that lived values and norms of ethical conduct, more than documents alone, are the true litmus test of the support for a mission statement, the follow-through on a strategic plan, or the determination of how financial resources will be allocated.

As congregations and societies at large have become more complex and diffuse, and beliefs and religious practice a more individual matter of choice, the process of self-definition and goal setting has become crucial to enshrining core values of any faith in the shared experience of religious community. I have had conversations with community leaders over the years who have shared how the process of developing a mission statement or statement of principles has reengaged their membership in the life of their community and has helped guide decisions throughout the organization or congregation. I have also spoken to those who feel it is an exercise on paper only. Either way, we demonstrate who we are and what our community stands for with every choice we make. The question the mission statement process poses to us is: "Are we consciously or reactively growing and deepening who we are as a community?"

Within the Jewish tradition, the concept of *brit* (covenant) has been a powerful binding force. We are in a covenantal relationship both with the Divine and with each other, and who we say we are reflects our commitment to the values that we strive to integrate in our relationships with one another. In North America, where multiple religious and cultural expressions exist in a marketplace of ideas, the process of developing a clear and frequently revisited definition for voluntary faith community can help keep us connected to the richness of our heritage, creatively responsive to the present, and conscious of the future we wish to live into. In this way the covenant of a former time becomes, to paraphrase David in the books of Samuel, "representative of the living God" as expressed in contemporary communities of choice.

One example of a contemporary version of integrating the traditional Jewish idea of a covenant in an egalitarian and inclusive congregational setting today was developed by the leadership of the Jewish Reconstructionist Congregation of Evanston, Illinois. The Jewish Reconstructionist Congregation (JRC) involved the entire community in a process to develop a statement that helps define membership beyond dues and financial exchange. This "community covenant" was accepted by the congregation and is part of new member packages as well. If we are to cultivate a sense of belonging in our faith communities that is not only linked to what it costs to be a member or a fee for service approach, such statements help define membership as mutual relationship that contains, but is not limited to, monetary exchange.

Jewish Reconstructionist Congregation Community Covenant: 2000

Jewish Reconstructionist Congregation is more than the total of individuals who belong to an institution. At JRC we deeply value our relationships with one another and with our community. As Jewish tradition teaches, with any sacred relationship there is a sense of *brit* (covenant)—a shared understanding of our mutual commitment to one another.

Thus, our JRC Community Covenant is a document that will help us explore the specific nature of our congregation's responsibilities to its members, and in turn, our own responsibilities to the community that is JRC. Characteristically, we consider this to be a work in progress, realizing that we will continue to study, modify, and interpret our covenant in ways we deem appropriate to meet the ever-changing needs of our community.

Our Community Covenant is not intended as a set of enforceable requirements or standards with which to judge our individual members. Rather, it is a general expression of our own communal and personal expectations. We recognize and cherish the diversity of our membership and understand that each member will interpret and express the terms of our covenant in different ways and at

different times. It is our hope that this *brit* will help us to understand the true meaning of community and especially to understand what JRC truly means to us.

1. *Members can expect JRC to help them understand and feel an
    attachment to Jewish people as a whole, around the world and
    across time.*
    JRC expects its members to acknowledge their attachment
    to Jewish people with pride and personal commitment.
2. *Members can expect JRC to teach and practice the values and
    virtues of Reconstructionist Judaism.*
    JRC expects its members to learn, uphold, and model those
    values and virtues.
3. *Members can expect JRC to provide spiritual guidance through
    our rabbi, cantor, and lay leadership.*
    JRC expects its members to make Jewish spirituality a per-
    sonal priority.
4. *Members can expect JRC to provide a warm, welcoming, and
    inclusive community.*
    JRC expects its members to respect our diversity and wel-
    come newcomers to our community with a spirit of accep-
    tance.
5. *Members can expect JRC to provide a diverse array of congre-
    gational activities.*
    JRC expects its members to participate and become involved
    in congregational activities as much as possible.
6. *Members can expect JRC to provide quality Jewish educational
    opportunities to children and adults alike.*
    JRC expects its members to take Jewish learning seriously.
7. *Members can expect JRC to provide serious and challenging*
    b'nai mitzvah *training.*
    JRC expects its members to take their children's education
    seriously and to participate in it.
8. *Members can expect JRC to provide spiritually moving and
    meaningful religious services.*
    JRC expects its members to enhance our worship by offer-
    ing their presence, participation, skills, and willingness to
    learn.
9. *Members can expect JRC to provide them with a Jewish com-
    munal outlet for* tikkun olam *(social action) involvement.*
    JRC expects its members to lend their experience, knowledge,

and energy to help us in our efforts to transform and heal
the world.

10. *Members can expect JRC to maintain the highest level of financial responsibility.*

    JRC expects its members to meet their financial obligations
    fully and generously.

11. *Members can expect JRC to welcome and respect their input and concerns about JRC.*

    JRC expects its members to be forthcoming with their concerns and advice.

12. *Members can expect JRC to provide opportunities for congregational leadership.*

    JRC expects its members to be generous with their time and
    energy to help our community become the best it can be.

Bringing Jewish values and integrating or adapting traditional concepts into the life of our communities can, as the JRC covenant demonstrates, keep the purpose, benefits, and expectations of membership in our congregations or organizations the responsibility of each generation.

MISSION STATEMENTS

Why am I recommending you develop articulated statements, reviewed every few years on a community-wide basis, that accurately define who your community is, what it aims to do, and how it aims to do it? Certainly not as a make-work project, when effort and attention is needed elsewhere. As it pertains to the subject matter of this book, we need to have clarity of purpose to inform our decisions around the collection and allocation of financial resources in our congregations or organizations.

If there are questions about how to spend money, or about competing programmatic and committee needs, is the budget driven by the loudest voice, the largest donor, the most energized individual or subgroup? If, for example, *tikkun olam* (social action) is not part of our stated mission, but a committed project of only one individual or a small group, and not embraced in the mission of the community as a whole, then what happens when that individual or group leaves the community, burns out, or switches financial allocation to another project? What happens to social action? Does the board look to other areas of the operating budget or to the clergy and volunteers to maintain the programming and funding in this area, or does it disappear from our consciousness and offerings? Having a community-wide and owned mission asks us to own such commitments on an ongoing basis and define the following:

- Who is to be served? (definition of membership internally and externally)
- What is to be served? (religious path or movement, spiritual life, and so forth)
- How will it be served? (services, programs, and so forth)

Having a shared understanding of what we stand for and whom we serve is not only the luxury of a society of abundant choice and resources, as the following text from the Warsaw Ghetto in 1940s, Second World War Poland demonstrates:

> Our association is not organized for the purpose of attaining power . . . our goal is to gradually rise above the noise and tumult of the world, by steady incremental steps. It is not consistent with our goals to hand out awards to who is advanced and who lags behind. The whole premise of our group is the vast potential for both baseness and elevation . . . but our potential for holiness is very great. Holiness is our key and primary value; honors and comparisons serve no useful purpose. . . . The whole point of our association is to love each other as much as possible. . . . The techniques available to a group are qualitatively different than what an individual can hope to attain.
>
> It is important for us to be explicit and clear that our society accepts into its ranks only those individuals who share these concerns. If people know in their hearts that they are not similarly burdened with these concerns, we ask that they do not join our group. They will harm themselves and others. Their presence will serve as a distraction to the rest of the group, whose hearts and minds are sincerely focused on this work.[1]

Even in the most difficult and life-threatening times, Rabbi Shapira asks what the opening biblical quote of this chapter advises—articulate a vision or be defined by internal impulses and external influences. You may want to study the JRC covenant and the Rabbi Shapira text at a board meeting or congregational retreat and see what ideas and feelings they inspire.

CREATING AND UPDATING A MISSION STATEMENT

Mission statements or "statements of principles" articulate the shared values of a given community. The process of articulating what the community stands for and offers can help bring greater cohesion, self-definition, and aid in planning for the future.

The committee that drafts your mission statement should be representative of your community as a whole and its internal diversity. Ideally, include or draw from lay leaders and staff, ritual, education, social action, and membership or outreach chairs, singles, parents, men and women, diverse sexual orientations, young adults, midlife and senior members, and so forth. Aim for a committee of seven or nine people that is representative of the demographics of your community or organization.

Begin by agreeing on a chairperson and defining your process. Read and discuss mission statements from other communities or organizations of your type. Agree on who will actually write the mission statement. While writing is usually a solitary pursuit that cannot be done effectively by a committee, it is a process that is most successful when the writer receives uncritical feedback, supportive guidance, and concrete suggestions. Some ways of approaching this include the following:

1. Brainstorm together in session, with the writer making notes.
2. Hold a collective session, with the writer working on the results afterward and returning to the group. The writer will work in concert with the committee. Decide whether the writer will receive feedback from one or two designated people or the entire committee during the writing process. When the first draft of the statement has been written, it should be presented to the committee for review and commentary. Whether the committee as a whole subsequently reviews it in its entirety, or in smaller sections by smaller groups, the process should be clearly articulated before one word is written. The final draft, which is not really final until it is approved, should be reviewed by the entire committee. Evaluation criteria includes the following:

   • Is your mission statement clear? Ask people who have not been involved in the writing process to read it and then tell you what it says.

- Is your mission feasible, motivational, and distinctive? Will your current and prospective membership buy into it?
- Is it a statement of accountability that is clearly articulated?
- What does it ask of the members of your community?
- What religious values in general, and of your denomination in particular, does it articulate about sacred community? Does it address critical ongoing or emerging community needs and responses?
- Does it provide the sense of direction now and for the foreseeable future that you want it to? (A mission statement should be reviewed every three to five years.)
- What is the role of the mission statement in communal governance?
- Where is your mission statement to be published (congregational or organizational brochure, in preamble to bylaws, policy manual, and so forth)?
- When you compare your mission statement with your income and expenditures, do you allocate and spend in accordance with your mission or do your stated values and your financial practices operate in separate universes?
- How can a mission statement be used as a tool for values clarification and decision making? How can the language of these documents be continually reinforced in the life of the community?

Here is a values-clarification exercise as part of rewriting a mission statement that I have adapted from Rabbi Toba Spitzer of Dorshei Tzedek, Newton, Massachusetts. It gives you an example of applying Jewish values and participatory process to engaging your congregation or organization in what its reasons for being and foundations for action are.

At the time, the congregational focus was on thinking about its future in light of planning for growth in membership. Rabbi Spitzer began with some study of texts from the writings of Jewish philosopher Martin Buber that have to do with community and the need for something at the center of true community. The "center" here is in terms of the congregation's mission, that which holds a community together. Buber writes:

The true community does not arise through people having feelings for one another (though indeed not without it), but through, first, their taking their stand in living mutual relation with a living Center, and, second, their being in living mutual relation with one another. The second has its source in the first, but is not given when the first alone is given. Living mutual relation includes feelings, but does not originate with them. The community is built up out of living mutual relation, but the builder is the living effective Center.[2]

Then, we divided up into groups of six or so, and each group got a stack of little cards with values on them, including one blank card. Each group had to come to agreement and choose six out of the seventeen values or practices that they thought were most important for the congregation. We then wrote a paragraph describing the essence of what the congregation stands for based on those six values. This is the original list of values we generated and following, the process we used to choose the values most important to us and write a formative mission statement:

1. *Kedushah* (Holiness)
2. *Hachnasat Orchim* (Welcoming and Inclusivity)
3. *Limud Torah* (Jewish Learning)
4. *Tefillah* (Prayer and Spiritual Practice)
5. Democracy
6. *Tzedek* (Justice)
7. *Kehillah* (Commitment to Community)
8. *Gemilut Hasadim* (Covenantal Caring; for example, visiting the sick and comforting mourners)
9. Ethical and Ritual Practice
10. *B'tzelem Elohim* (In God's Image or "treating all people with dignity")
11. *Menuchah* (Rest and Renewal)
12. *L'dor v'dor* (Connecting the Generations)
13. *Hiddur Mitzvah* (Beauty)
14. *Simcha* (Joy and Celebration)
15. *Bal Tashchit* (Avoiding Waste)
16. *Rodef Shalom* (Pursuing Peace)
17. Diversity

Dorshei Tzedek: Values and Mission

Step One: As a group, choose six of the seventeen Jewish values or
practices cards that you think are most important to or representative of your congregation (there is one blank card if you wish to add
something that you think is missing from the list).
   Please write your six values here:

   1.
   2.
   3.
   4.
   5.
   6.

Step Two: Using your six values or practices, and referring to your own
community's mission statement or statement of principles, either:

a) Write a paragraph or two describing an ideal week at your
congregation.

                                   or

b) Write a one- or two- (no longer!) paragraph mission statement
that reflects those values.

Step Three: Share what you have written with a *hevrutah* (study
partner). What are the similarities and differences? How close or far
from your partner's experience of your shared community is your
own statement?

Step Four: Have a large printout or overhead of your existing mission statement. How do these Jewish values–based statements compare with your mission statement? What changes need to be adopted
that will more fully reflect the existing and hoped for reality?

Step Five: The results of this exercise and some of the mission statement options will be communicated to the entire congregation for
further input. Subsequently, the committee responsible for generating the final mission statement will use this feedback to craft two or
three final options for the congregation to vote on as a whole.

The entire congregation is involved in determining the mission and values of the congregation—the long-term goals and desires. The board is then empowered to make decisions and establish committees that would implement and work toward those goals. There is then a direct connection from the process and philosophical work to the values set that should be informing the finance committee, the budget process, programming, how revenue is generated and invested, and how money is spent and distributed within the congregation. By thoughtfully engaging as leaders and as a community in an ongoing fashion about your mission and the vision you have for achieving it, you create the opportunity to determine a bottom line that integrates values with financial direction.

3

Money as a Spiritual Tool

Planning and Budgeting

The Divine plan makes it necessary to devote time to providing
for one's own material needs.
—Babylonian Talmud, *Berachot* 356

Planning is one of the most important functions in synagogue life,
and yet it is one rarely addressed in a systematic, nonreactive way.
Once we have understood and clarified our values, and created a
mission statement that embodies them, we then look to create a
plan to fulfill that mission. There are a number of good resources
available on the planning and budgeting processes themselves. What
I want to underscore in this chapter are some of the key elements to
keep in mind as we go forward in a planning process and in values-
based budgeting.

As a starting exercise, imagine how you would respond if you
arrived at your congregational board or general meeting and found
that an anonymous gift of $50,000 was given to your congregation
or organization—no strings attached. How would you, as an entrusted leader with fiduciary responsibility, direct the use of that
money? What values would you use to prioritize how you used the
money? What needs are most pressing? Is there in fact a sense of
purpose and direction that informs how your budget is spent and
allocated?

May we all be blessed by such unexpected opportunities! Beginning planning and budgeting by examining your community's mission and values is one way of trying to live out your community's

dreams, without merely responding to presenting issues and expenses as they arise, whether blessings or challenges.

A long-range plan serves as a framework for determining goals, objectives, priorities, policies, budgets, and programming over a specified period of time. By first establishing the congregation's guiding principles (such as vision, mission, values, and areas of focus), then analyzing the community's strengths and weaknesses, strategies can be created to build on existing strengths and close the gaps to fulfill the guiding principles and reach the community's vision.[1] The planning process does not end with the delivery of a long-range or strategic plan. Planning is an ongoing dimension to maintaining and growing sacred community.

Planning is also vital to encouraging and managing growth and ongoing change in the congregational or organizational system. By growth I do not necessarily mean quantitative; I firmly believe growth is an ongoing dynamic in any community, regardless of size or years of existence. I see growth and change as reflections of the Divine presence that is the process of life itself. Growth and change happen whether we put our minds to it or not. This can be emotional, intellectual, and spiritual in nature, as well as the more obvious physical changes we may see on the surface individually or as a community. Planning is an attempt to move beyond a reactive stance to the reality of change and growth around us.

At the same time, growth can also be understood in quantitative terms: number of member households, staff size, variety of programs, array of resources, and all areas of congregational life. Most faith communities want to grow in ways that do not compromise or sacrifice their reasons for coming together to form a religious community. Growth can bring greater diversity, additional resources, and more opportunity for participation for both current and new members. Growth can also challenge the feeling of intimacy or levels of communication in a community, and left unchecked, growth strains preexisting capacities. An effective and inclusive planning process can help reduce the stress, fear, and uncertainty when dealing with all these issues of growth.

The planning process is not an insurance against crisis nor is it a guarantee. At times congregational leaders and professional staff will go through a planning process and assume the future is assured. Planning means working with the variables that present themselves in the life of a community or organization. It also means anticipating future needs or goals. The ceiling may spring a leak or an electrical fire may give new meaning to an existing capital campaign. A beloved clergy may become ill or move for family or career reasons.

Think of the experience of the Israelites at Sinai. A world-changing plan for sacred living in the form of the Ten Commandments and the initial laws governing community and individual life are developed. God and Moses are on the planning committee, but the most profound social-spiritual blueprint will be the work of a generation (and more!). I am not trying to imply that our congregational plans and budgets are operating on the same level or will take 40 years or generations to unfold, but plans and budgets of our communities are also the ground on which our values and collective spiritual aspirations are played out.

Ultimately, planning means trying to make things happen *for* the congregation, instead of letting things happen *to* the congregation. Without an ongoing process of planning that is accepted and understood by the leadership, the synagogue tends to govern itself through crisis management. Thus decisions and polices are made in a time crunch and are often spurred by real-life situations. The community is not afforded the opportunity to take time to make decisions or to think of issues in the abstract and ideal instead of the personal and acute.

Avoiding burnout and crises in the area of communal staffing needs, both professional and support, is another goal of good planning. A strategic plan can be helpful for congregations examining the need for an executive director or increasing the rabbinic presence from part-time to full-time. A Jewish values-based approach to staffing includes fair remuneration and responsible employee benefits packages.

The object of a plan such as this is not to wait for the unanticipated, but foresee the needs of the future in the present. Some important questions to ask in the course of planning include the following:

- Who will lead the process?
- Will you develop the plan in a group or committee that represents a cross section of age, class, gender, sexual orientation, family structure, length of membership, and other membership variables?
- Who will do the research? (including a description and evaluation of the current status of the congregation)

- Can the planning committee or consultant team lead positively and without division?
- Are the planners actually empowered to develop a plan or will it be a make-work project that the community, board, rabbi, and other key staff are not in support of?
- Who is defining the needs and priorities and what process will be used to define these?
- What are the "felt" needs and what are the practical needs?
- What issues need to be handled sensitively?
- What areas need to be promoted for the health of the community's future?
- How will the communications be organized and delivered throughout? (such as town hall or parlor meetings, newsletter and electronic communications, planning group retreats, community questionnaires)
- How will you evaluate the results and impact of your plan?
- What will you pay for and what will you keep as volunteer positions and activities? (For example, do you want volunteers moving chairs and stuffing envelopes or learning to lead services, develop policy, and so on?)
- As the plan is set into action, what will be the effects on the various aspects of the congregational system (such as religious school, ritual life and needs, staffing, physical plant, finances, programming, membership, and so on) if the plan is successful?

Your community simultaneously shapes and reflects the values they live by. Planning should be vision driven, based on the mission of the community and supported by covenantal governing documents and policies you have already enshrined. As faith communities, we have the opportunity and, dare I say, obligation to help people really look at what is behind or beneath their individual beliefs and actions.

CONGREGATIONAL SYSTEMS

When doing any form of planning we can often become focused on particular areas of congregational or organizational life and forget to keep our eyes on the community as a whole. A helpful perspective to keep is that of a systems approach to congregational life. The Alban Institute has a number of publications that explore and explain congregational systems. For a Jewish perspective I draw here from a landmark report, *The Rabbinic-Congregation Relationship: A Vision for the 21st Century*, edited by Rabbi Richard Hirsh, executive director of the Reconstructionist Rabbinical Association.

The report offers that beginning in the 1960s and '70s "systems theory" emerged in the field of family therapy and then spread into the nonprofit and business world. A systems approach looks at the totality of a social organization and the interaction within it. This approach recognizes that the parts interact organically, with the whole being greater than the sum of its parts. As applied to congregational life, a systems approach takes into account the interaction of the various parts of the community and their impact on each other, rather than looking only at individual roles and functions.

Rabbi Mordecai Kaplan, a leading Jewish thinker of the twentieth century, called this the principle of "organic reciprocity"—meaning that the whole acts upon the part, and the part in turn acts upon the whole. From a Jewish perspective, this also implies mutual responsibility and ethical conduct that is part of a spiritual covenant between individuals, between human beings and God, and within communities themselves. There are thus opportunities for learning core Jewish spiritual values, and the cause and effect of behavior of individuals and groups, in using a systems approach to understand congregational life. Kaplan writes:

> The human being is not a self-contained atom, but is the product of the biological, historical and social forces that operate in the group to which he belongs. . . . What has been said of words in relation to their context is true of human beings in relation to their communities; they are not "pebbles in juxtaposition"; they have only a communal existence; the meaning of each interpenetrates the others.[2]

Systems tend to resist change when first introduced, or when change is made conscious as it is occurring. This includes change that is viewed as positive as well as negative. A systems approach also does not deny that difficult people and problems are real issues for individuals and congregations. Systems theory asserts that reactive patterns and unconscious agreements or "understandings" about how people are supposed to be in community needs to be explored as a whole. Identifying these behaviors, naming them without attacking or judging each other, and strategizing how to speak to concerns that may come up in light of proposed change from parts of the system where these behaviors are entrenched, can be helpful in making a proposed plan effective in the long run.

Individuals, of course, play a role in and affect a system, as do the subsystems of the congregation (such as the individuals on the fundraising committee for a capital campaign, the volunteer and professional teachers in the school, the members of the rabbi-liaison or evaluation committee, and so on). The rabbi, along with other staff and lay leadership, plays a primary role in the congregational system by setting and following through on the agenda in response to the congregation's circumstances.[3]

A Systems Approach to Planning

Let's look at an extended example of a systems approach to a plan for growth. Instead of only focusing on a certain number of new member households, and the revenue and expenses involved with this, we would look at the impact of moderate growth on every aspect of the congregation, in adding "x" number of households. This example is not intended to cover every area of congregational life or ask every related question. I am assuming there has been a process to clarify the mission and values of the community and that due process has been given to arrive at the plan.

Hebrew School

How will the Hebrew school need to be expanded to meet "x" number of additional children? Will new staff be required? Will classes need to meet additional days? How will this affect parent carpooling? How will the timing of additional classes affect the families, the levels of concentration the student will have, and the amount of homework students will be given? Will additional classes affect adult education or other programs in the congregation? Will there be costs related to classroom dividers, new classrooms, or rented classroom trailers?

Ritual Life

Will there be a cap on how many bar or bat mitzvahs there are per year (such as limiting the number of Shabbat morning bar or bat mitzvahs and requiring Shabbat afternoon or weekday bar or bat mitzvahs)? How many years of study will be required ahead of the event? How will increased membership affect the tone and participation in worship services? How will new members be integrated into services? Will alternative services be needed for those regulars for whom keeping a sense of community would necessitate a separate service as an alternative to the larger service with an influx of visitors? How will the increase in demand for space for all lifecycle rituals be navigated? What time demand increase will this require of the rabbi and other staff? What other areas of their work will be deprioritized to accommodate the increased demand on their time, or will additional clergy and staff be required to minister and administer the increase in membership? Will the existing worship space be sufficient to accommodate the anticipated growth? If current High Holy Days take place within the existing sanctuary or rented space, will a new space be required for additional members?

STAFFING

How will additional demands on the rabbi's time from an increase in member households in general, or bar and bat mitzvahs in particular, be handled? Is additional clergy needed to augment increased membership? How about school and office staffing? Will additional maintenance, such as increased cleaning, setup, and breakdown, be required? What additional programming will be added to meet the increase in membership, and who will deliver and administer the programs? What process (involving staff or lay volunteers) will be established to integrate new members into the community and help long-standing members still feel connected to the community? Should *havurot* (small affinity groups) be formed to make sure new and existing members integrate and remain connected to each other? Who will oversee these subgroups?

PHYSICAL PLANT

If space is rented, what are the cost factors for increased usage? If owned, how will fuller use of the building be managed? Are programs in private homes an option? Is the space, including the kitchen, equipped for larger events or more frequent use? Is parking space and traffic flow sufficient, particularly for Hebrew school days? Does the plan include provisions for wear and tear?

FINANCES

What is the predicted growth in revenue, as well as capital and operating costs increases? School expenses tend to grow faster than tu-
ition, part of which is usually subsidized by the congregation at large
based on the Jewish value of educating young people. Will there be
additional capital outlays such as desks, chairs, books, kitchen im-
provements, carpets, repainting, etc? Will there be an increase in
need for storage?

These are just some of the questions one might ask in a planning
process from the perspective that views the congregation as an organic whole with interdependent and interactive parts. Grounding a
planning process in a Jewish values–based approach, means keeping
any planning process and ultimate plan connected to the basic purpose or mission of the community, as well as identifying principles
that will guide the planners in the actions that are recommended.

BUDGETING

We create budgets for the same reason we create other plans—so
that the use of our resources will be consistent with our values and
priorities. I will not get into detail about the mechanics and how-tos
of budgeting here, except to underscore the following themes: a
budget is a direct expression of what the congregation or organization values and how it uses financial resources to realize its mission.
In the final analysis there may never be enough resources for everything we want to do, but even if we do not increase our capacity, we
can align our resource expenditures with our purpose as a community, and make sure we use the resources we have to support our
highest values.

All budgets have a revenue side and an expense side. In a values-
based budgeting process, it is often the expense side that leads. Of
course, one may go through periods of limiting expenses, but the
question of what is behind these limitations is still a question of
values (for example, why are expenses being cut in one area or the
other and what commitment, or lack thereof, does this reflect in a
particular area of congregational life?). Returning to the section on
text and tradition from chapter 1 can help serve as a reminder for

many of the Jewish perspectives on money as a spiritual tool in building sacred community.

Budgeting begins with a clear institutional vision that asks:

- Who are we?
- What are our objectives?
- What must be done to achieve our goals?

The budget committee is not responsible for determining the synagogue's priorities and direction. It receives that information from the board or executive committee and, with its unique expertise, provides projections, offers options, and explains the consequences of the various choices to the decision makers. In small communities many of the same people may sit on both committees.

You can take the pulse of how your own community deals with money and finances by asking yourselves the following questions:

- Do we discuss money issues in an ongoing way in our faith community, or only when we are in financial crises?
- Where in our congregational or organizational system do we deal with money openly and where only when there is a real problem?
- Do we feel trust in our leadership and their allocation of funds or do we question how money is being taken in and spent?

The communication and trust climate around financial issues in your community will affect the budgetary process in its formation and implementation. Are the questions of "What can we afford to do?" and "What can we not afford to do?" the only budgetary questions being asked? Or do you also ask, "What does Jewish tradition and a commitment to holiness in our actions ask of us in the allocation of our communal resources? Where are we willing to take a leap of faith (for example, hire the full-time rabbi, build a youth chapter, look to hire the best qualified teachers)?"

BUDGET TIPS

While the Alban Institute and the major Jewish movements have good resources about budgeting, here are a few reminders as you move forward in this critical task of implementing your congregation's or organization's mission and objectives.

- In the budgeting process, break down costs so people can connect the small expenses to the larger sums and understand what events cost, how finances are managed, and how programs that are part of the mission of the community touch their lives and are valued. Summarize these costs for presentation, with an introduction of how the budget reflects the mission, priorities, and Jewish and general values.

- Link the budget to cash flow, charting when expenditures and revenues tend to occur. This can avoid the "early summer panic"—when dues have been spent and income is not yet flowing in for independent High Holy Day revenue and annual membership dues.

- Even though most congregations offer education as an additional service for a fee, no household pays for the full cost of education. Subsidizing education in a Jewish community is seen as the outcome of a core Jewish value, a *mitzvah* or "sacred duty" as part of communal responsibility. How is this reflected in your budget? Does your membership understand the real cost of education and to what degree this reflects what you stand for?

- Make sure you factor in expenses such as compensation time, clergy sabbaticals, parental leave, vacation, conservation and environmentally friendly upgrading costs, respectful wages for caretaking staff, teachers, and so on.

- Try to avoid wasting money on cheap short-term decisions (for example, bargain computer systems), and ensure proper investment in infrastructure by doing it right the first time.

- A great looking budget may have months of crises built into it because of miscalculated cash flow!

All of our resources are finite—we have a limited number of staff, we have a limited quantity of volunteer hours, our buildings have a limited amount of space, and so on. Beginning with the Jewish view that money is a tool to live out our commitment to justice, to holy action in the world, our decisions on allocating these limited resources should reflect and be directed by our core values and priorities. While the amount of financial resources may go through cycles of greater or lesser availability, what we stand for is evident in how and on what we spend. Attitudes of abundance or scarcity are not defined by the actual amount of money available. With an eye to the patterns that may influence our choices and attitudes in the budgeting process, we can look consciously for ways of making the budget reflect our mission and objectives.

In the budgetary process we have the opportunity to look at how we can remain proactive and nonreactive to keeping a spiritual perspective of abundance and trust in God's presence in our choices without making monetary decisions that undermine the long-term viability of our communities or the mission, the Jewish practices we follow, and the values we aspire to live out.

A Purpose Chart: Putting Mission, Values, Planning, and Budgeting Together

One innovative way to help people ground planning and budgeting in their congregational or organizational mission is through the use of a "purpose chart," developed by Howard Ellegant, a consultant who assists organizations and companies to improve performance, projects, and products, and member of the Jewish Reconstructionist Congregation in Evanston, Illinois.

This exercise helps a community strategize future activities and place current activities in the context of their mission. It demonstrates how current activities and programs and their cost can be related to the congregation's mission and values and sets up the conversation for allocating resources to new programs based on the mission. I suggest doing this exercise as a board or financial committee as a way of putting the ideas of this chapter into action.

After seeing how money is being spent and whether the community is effectively raising, allocating, and spending its resources in light of its mission and values, a key element in this process is to prioritize. The instructions and graph on the following page take you through this process step by step.

Using the Congregational Purpose Chart to Plan

Time Needed: 100 minutes
Setup: 10 minutes

Purpose

- To use the purpose chart to strategize and to plan for future activities.

Mission

Our congregation helps its members in their desire to fulfill the principles of Judaism as a way of life.

Purpose/Vision Elements	Be a caring community			Share commitment to make Judaism meaningful		Serve the larger Jewish community		
	1. Recognize and respond to the diversity of our community.	2. Serve the larger world.	3. Remain a financially viable institution.	4. Create an atmosphere to merge ancient Jewish traditions with modern thinking in a creative and meaningful way.	5. Encourage members to take an active role in congregation life.	6. Prepare and develop the next generation of Jews.	7. Create the Jewish experience in our area.	8. Share the Jewish experience in our area.
Strategy								
Performance Measure and Target								
Current Activities or Programs								
Current Activity Cost								

Why? →   ← How?

Congregational Purpose Chart

The purpose chart links purpose and cost to present a picture of resources allocated and expended to fulfill congregational mission.

(Data adapted from several congregational long-range plans.)

- To place current activities in the context of the congregation's mission.
- To demonstrate how current activities/programs and their cost can be related to congregation's mission.
- To set up the conversation for allocating resources to new programs based on the congregation's mission.

ACTIVITY

Invite people into groups of three or four to explore different aspects of congregational activities, or work together as one group if you are less than seven participants. Hand out the purpose chart and direct people to go through the following steps in their working groups:

Based on the mission of your community (if you do not have an articulated mission statement, see chapter 2): (1) create a strategy; (2) create a target and performance measure; and (3) identify a *current* activity or program that fulfills the purpose. Then: (4) prepare a report of your work to the whole group.

SMALL-GROUP WORK (50 MINUTES)

1. *Identify current activities or programs.*

- Assess who is doing what, what is being done, and how it is being done in the congregation.

   Example
   Purpose or Vision Element—"Encourage members to take an active role in congregation life."
   - List who is currently in leadership roles, how long they have been in those roles, and in what areas of congregational life they have shown leadership. How is the next leadership group developed?

2. *Create a strategy.*

- This is a process for reaching an outcome that would demonstrate the congregation had succeeded in fulfilling or moving closer to realizing its purpose. You should be able to monitor and gauge its achievement.
- *Quickly* brainstorm 2 to 4 strategies that would achieve each purpose. Rate them as "easy to do," "a stretch," and "it'll never happen."

Example
Purpose or Vision Element—"Engage members to take an active role in congregation life."
Strategy—"Create a training program for prospective congregational leaders."

3. *Create a performance measure and target.*

- For each strategy, identify at least one way the congregation could measure the performance of the strategy and one or more possible targets.
- Select *one* strategy with its associated performance measure and target to put on your chart.

Example
Purpose or Vision Element—"Encourage members to take an active role in congregation life."
Strategy—"Training program for prospective congregational leaders."
Performance Measure—Number of new board or committee members trained or number of new chairs or leaders of programs/projects. Target=100 percent by "x" date.

REPORT TO LARGE GROUP (**20** MINUTES)

(Skip if working as one small group.)

Each subgroup prepares a short report to the whole group:

1. Name your group's purpose/vision element.
2. Identify your group's "easy to do," "a stretch," and "it'll never happen" strategies.
3. Name the strategy you chose to include on the chart.
4. Identify the progress measure and target for the strategy you included on the chart.
5. Identify the current activity or program that fulfills the purpose or vision and the current costs related to those activities.

REVIEWING THE SUBGROUP WORK AND PROCESS (**20** MINUTES)

Discuss the following questions:

- What similarities did you notice in the group reports? What differences?
- What in the reports got your attention or excited you? Why?
- What questions do you have for any of the groups?
- What questions do you have about the purpose chart?
- What will you take away from this for your congregation's ongoing planning and budgeting process?
- What about the process seems easy?
- Where did you expect to have the most difficulty?
- What information does this way of planning and budgeting bring to the table that is currently lacking in your congregation?
- What Jewish or congregational values does this planning and budgeting method support?

A Last Word

The planning process is a framework within which policies are formed, budget and fundraising goals are set, programming and staff needs are projected. Planning ideally focuses on the programs and services the congregation will be called upon to provide in the future. A good long-range plan can provide a clear direction for a community seeking growth, while at the same time trying to preserve those aspects of its program that it values most highly.

To this end it provides an opportunity to set up focus groups or survey the congregation every few years to make sure the plan and the lived experience and needs of the community are in alignment, or examine where the community may need to shift and realign if there has been a drifting away from the core mission and values. The process of planning, systems thinking, and values-based budgeting can keep our actions in alignment with the view that money is a spiritual tool for building holy and whole communities.

4

SUSTAINING SACRED COMMUNITY

From the Half-Shekel to Contemporary Dues

We laid upon ourselves obligations; to charge ourselves one-third
of a shekel yearly for the service of the House of our God.
—Neh. 10:33

In every synagogue members pay dues, but there are a variety of
synagogue dues structures. The focus of this chapter is to enable
your community to clarify its values and harmonize your
congregation's dues structures and policies with those values. I am
increasingly impressed by the creative ways that many congregations are implementing fair-share dues structures while not only
maintaining but actually increasing their revenues and ability to offer meaningful programming and adequate professional staff. I have
also seen many congregations that once had flat dues structures with
maybe only a couple of categories (family and single, for example)
begin to diversify their dues categories to meet the needs of complex family systems, age, economic resource differentials, and outreach to new and unaffiliated members. Some communities even
have hybrid dues structures, with an obligatory minimum and additional income percentages built in.

Each community, according to its scale of mission and services,
denominational philosophy, and the influence of geographic, demographic, and economic factors, will develop its own formula for
establishing and collecting dues. A model that has been historically
successful is not necessarily best for today. Even when a
congregation's dues structure works well for the members and

53

community as a whole, the way new members are introduced to their financial obligations and how money is discussed throughout the congregational system has enormous impact. The impact can determine whether the concept of consumer oriented fee-for-service mentality is evoked, or covenantal, values-based membership in a faith community is enshrined.

EARLY MODELS

Since developing as a people after the exodus from Egypt, the most common method of raising funds in Jewish community has been through taxation.[1]

At the very birth of the Jewish people in the exodus from Egypt, Jews traditionally paid a minimum tax to support the establishment and maintenance of their ritual, sacred center, their leadership, and later the Temples where the priests made their sacrifices. They also provided a share of their tribal allocation to the Levites, so that the Levites could focus on the needs of the sacrificial cult. Thus there was an obligatory contribution to support the *avodah* (sacred service). The Jewish spirit of practicality is expressed in the rabbinic saying, "Where there is no bread, there can be no Torah, Where there is no Torah, there will be no bread." [2]

A variety of historical events and *halakhik* adaptations over many centuries have affected and developed the biblical idea of stewardship and social responsibility for the community in which Jews belonged, and while not going thoroughly into them here, I do want to highlight a few themes. As Rabbinic Judaism developed from 70 BCE onwards, after the destruction of the Second Temple, the rabbis helped systematize the flow and allocation of resources according to core values, including holiness, community building, compassionate action, and service to God. In the Middle Ages, *parnaseem* (the Jewish community's leaders) were often asked to raise the government's taxes and they also developed a process to charge a separate *tzedekah* (Jewish tax). This money was collected and distributed by the *parnaseem* for the widow, orphan, and those in need. The modern synagogue has considerably more extensive financial needs and has taken on many tasks that the old synagogue never had. It is a *beit midrash* (a school), a *beit knesset* (community center), a social hall, a space to mark life-cycle events, a political center, a social service center (pastoral counseling, day care), and a youth center, to name a few. The costs of the infrastructure to meet these diverse needs have become substantial.

Each system of taxation reflects the religious, political, and social values that underlie the society in which the rates are assessed, as well as the exemptions allowed various groups. In today's world it is the values and priorities we hold individually, as well as a society, that in no small measure determine the degree of compliance with the demands of the tax collector or collection system, particularly in voluntaristic faith communities.

Meir Tamari, in *With All Your Possessions*, suggests that before the establishment of the modern welfare state, the Jewish view of society's responsibility for the needs of its members was founded on the axiomatic principle of collective responsibility. He goes on to say that traditionally a Jewish community managed its own fiscal system, whether as part of an independent commonwealth or within the bounds of a ruling nation or country, in accordance with Jewish legal and moral authority.

A Jewish community was obliged to finance Torah education, redemption of captives, *mikvaot* or "ritual immersion spaces," synagogues, cemeteries, and charities. These demands remained regardless of existing financial realities. From rabbinic until modern times, the *halakhik* system supported a variety of tax structures:

- *Halachah Shecheynim* (Law of neighbors)—Neighbors who share common facilities or property could obligate each other to finance common needs out of a joint fund. A municipal tax is an outgrowth of this neighborhood concept.
- *Din Ha'Ir* (Rule of the city)—Popularly elected officials could require citizens to finance projects for security and communal well-being. There was often a one-year grace period for newcomers, unless they bought property.
- *Dina Hamelekh* (Rule of the king)—Mishnah Sanhedrin 2:11 states that the king can appropriate land for the benefit of public needs.
- *Din Demalckutah Dina* (Rule of the state)—Following the obligations and legal system of the host nation (such as poll taxes at a flat rate, water, and taxes levied on income).

Tamari states that the Jewish view of collective responsibility moved beyond the idea of charity at the individual level that existed in other religious systems. In Judaism, taxation was introduced as a manifestation of the concept of the rights of the community and of the less fortunate. The setting up of a tax system institutionalized these rights and made participation in communal financing obligatory in addition to the voluntary charitable acts demanded by Judaism from the individual. Irrespective of the methods chosen to finance communal needs and the size of the communal budget, Jewish religious and legal institutions throughout the centuries maintained this vision of collective responsibility as a first principle—as axiomatic.[3]

LATER DEVELOPMENTS

The realities of oppression and autonomy experienced by Jewish communities of the fourteenth to eighteenth centuries brought a governance role to *kehillot* (the larger Jewish communal structure) that included collecting and distributing *tzedakah* funds. Rabbinic salaries were institutionalized in the fourteenth and fifteenth centuries, as anti-Semitic persecutions and expulsions expanded the rabbi's role from teacher and interpreter of Torah, to spiritual and political leader—even as rabbis and teachers were often cut off from outside means of earning a living. The first known salaried rabbi fled from Spain to Algiers in the fourteenth century. Since Jewish law traditionally forbade profiting from teaching Torah, he was contracted to receive *sekhar battalah* (compensation) for the loss of time associated with his duties, which became the *halakhik* basis for rabbinic salaries. Centuries later, the establishment of a tripartite national infrastructure by the Reform movement (a rabbinical seminary, a rabbinical association, and a congregational association) in nineteenth-century America created the need for major synagogue financing—and was emulated by each emerging denomination.[4]

Jewish religious teachings tried to create an ideological climate in which individual obligations to communal well-being were constantly reinforced. The last couple of centuries have given rise to the development of modern nation-states, the founding of Israel, the integration of Jews into mainstream North American culture, proliferation of Jewish organizations, charitable giving, and general membership through dues payments to Jewish community centers and synagogues.

SYNAGOGUE DUES

In Jewish life, an emphasis on community has historically been a core value. We are told to leave a portion of our field unharvested (Deut. 14:22). We are told to not glean the field or vineyards (Lev. 19:9). There is a traditional sense that a person is in a living dynamic covenant that should reflect generous giving. Even a recipient of *tzedakah* must give to those with less. The process of exploring our traditional sense of mutual obligation builds shared meaning.

Paying taxes is one of the obligations of citizenship. Synagogues have become a primary communal institution in terms of membership in the Jewish community. Dues are the way a congregation distributes the cost of its programs, salaries, and upkeep among its members. In this way, money and religious values intersect in an area that every member must experience, regardless of their religious practice, attendance at worship, or participation at communal events.

This also means the way the mission and values of a community and the way Jewish teaching are presented at this moment of financial commitment has great impact on the new member's experience of the community and what it stands for. When congregational representatives are communicating with new (and existing) members about obligations, they need to move between a marketing focus on the member's personal perceived needs and a prophetic focus on the community's traditional obligations. In marketing theory one can charge a price equal to the perceived value of the product. If leaders have increased the perceived value of membership, they can raise prices (dues). If they have declines in their perceived value, they, in theory, will either have to reduce prices or risk a decline in demand (declining membership). Perceived value is a very complex formulation.[5]

Yet synagogue membership includes a complex mix of specific service needs (religious school, lifecycle events, cemetery rights), self-esteem needs (participation, fellowship), and transcendent existential needs (spirituality, yearning for community), among others. In a consumer model, one might expect to pay only for the services one expects to use, need, or benefit from. In this model the individual's only responsibility is payment and the congregation's is provision of services. But we are not only paying a fee for services rendered when we join a synagogue, *havurah,* or a movement. Certainly, synagogues do not receive faith-based nonprofit status for being a one-stop religious warehouse.

Some congregations are addressing the need to demonstrate that membership is about more than money by having a skilled representative of the membership committee meet with prospects and just get to know them. They show concern. They encourage prospects to tell how they have progressed on their "Jewish journey" and slowly suggest ways the synagogue community might relate to them. Other congregations are defining membership using the traditional Jewish value of covenant by not taking any money for dues until the prospect has agreed to take on the responsibilities of membership as defined by the particular community.

If the conversation about dues focuses on monetary issues alone, dues are split off from their roots as a Jewish communal tax within a covenantal framework. In order for members to understand the holistic and sacred Jewish context of congregational dues, synagogues must clearly articulate their mission and how membership is defined and articulated in the ongoing life of the community.

CURRENT AND EMERGING MODELS

In the last couple of centuries, many synagogues and synagogue-movements were established in North America. The older movements (Orthodox, Conservative, and Reform), and more established congregations in general, have a history of meeting operating costs from dues and fund-raising, as well as a small percentage that have established endowments. Nearly 45 to 75 percent of their budgets are generally comprised of dues. Most Reconstructionist congregations formed in the 1960s onwards and newer communities operate with 65 to 80 percent of their budgets based on a variety of dues structures. The newer Jewish streams of Renewal and Secular Humanism, along with other emerging independent communities, are often more reliant on dues alone. For the newer communities the ratio may change over time with more comprehensive and creative approaches to fundraising.

There are two basic approaches to dues within Jewish congregations. Dues can be computed using demographic criteria, such as family configuration and age range. This has been the standard approach in contemporary Jewish life in North America, where synagogues have developed a variety of membership categories (such as single, senior, partnered, partnered with children). Dues can also be computed by income, using either a flat percentage or on a progressive scale (usually ranging around 1 to 3 percent). Despite some understandable fear about this approach, a number of congregations have reported increased income levels using this model. Some communities also include a voluntary dues line in the household membership form beyond flat or fair-share dues, so those who can afford more subsidize those who cannot.

Ethical mechanisms for assessing dues and requests for variances in dues that preserve the dignity and confidentiality of members are important to ensure fairness. Here the dignity of the individual must be balanced with the covenantal responsibility that goes with membership in a community. Communications about dues, especially if the system is undergoing change, is crucial.

In one informal rabbinic survey conducted by Rabbi Shoshana Kaminsky of Pittsburgh, the rabbis of congregations who follow a fair-share approach were enthusiastic about the results. Rabbi Kaminsky writes:

> Most congregations tie their adoption of the fair share system to a general reevaluation of the responsibilities and privileges of synagogue membership. In particular, members are encouraged to think of their synagogue dues as doing holy work, rather than as meeting expenses. Interestingly enough, even synagogue members whose fair share is a considerable sum are very enthusiastic about the program. They do not resent having to donate a large amount of money, because they know that everyone in their congregation is giving the same percentage of their income.

Implementing a fair share dues system did not appear to harm the finances of synagogues in any way; in fact, synagogues that faithfully adhere to an income-based dues system tend to experience a higher degree of financial security.

A number of colleagues noted their concern about the ways that congregations who do not follow an income-based system renegotiate dues for those unable to pay full dues. Several reported hearing from congregants who were forced into such a position that they were very humiliated by the experience, even when the synagogue officers were acting with the best of intentions. In small congregations, confidentiality is often compromised, and some less affluent members have even been ridiculed for their inability to pay full dues. Even when a well-thought-out system to renegotiate dues exists and is carefully followed, many Jews choose to withdraw from synagogue life rather than admit their financial limitations. Others feel that they hold lesser status in the congregation or are, in some way, beholden to the synagogue. The greatest benefit of a fair share dues system would therefore seem to be that it places all members, regardless of income, on an equal footing when it comes to making a meaningful contribution to their synagogue.[6]

The case study in chapter 7 will provide you with an example of a congregation's Jewish approach in shifting its dues policy and process. Even communities that retain flat dues structures are increasingly adding a variety of categories to attract new members and be more responsive to different socioeconomic needs (such as single, low-income elderly, newly married or partnered, multiple children). Some congregations resist raising dues out of concern for those with fewer financial resources. Some synagogues have begun creating categories such as "sustainer" or "patron," requesting that those who can pay an extra amount to compensate for the reality that 15 to 50 percent of members do not, or cannot, pay full dues. This demonstrates empathy for those in need while keeping the community focused on the needs of the congregation.

Other communities are looking at models that combine some basic obligatory contribution with a fair-share approach. The case study in chapter 7 is one such case of a Jewish values–based approach to reorganizing a congregational dues structure to include a flat, shared fee, plus a percentage of income as dues.

THE HIGH HOLY DAYS AND *TISHREI* MEMBERSHIPS

The language we use and the way money intersects with our communal structures reflect our values, especially at meaningful times in our individual and communal religious life. A colleague of mine in Philadelphia, Rabbi Marcia Prager, first sensitized me to the way we create meaning and perspectives on spiritual life and practice through the language we use to describe our religious experience. Rabbi Prager suggested that talking about "observing" and "attending" religious experiences distances us from the essential reason behind them. We do not "observe" holidays; rather, we celebrate them. We do not "attend" services; rather, we worship and *davenn* (pray). This led me to rethink the terminology of "purchasing tickets to attend High Holy Day services."

The "ticket" structure has been in place for many decades in synagogues in North America. It was developed as a way to determine anticipated attendance and required seating capacity for members at the most highly attended worship services in the Jewish year (Rosh Hashanah and Yom Kippur). "Tickets" have also acted as an annual marker of the financial obligations of membership, for security, and to allow nonmembers to attend these services for a fee that would support the ongoing life of the congregation.

In keeping with the Jewish view that dues are a sign of commitment and covenant, I floated the idea to a number of synagogue leaders I was consulting with, that they might consider offering membership in their communities for the month of Tishrei, in which the High Holy Days and Sukkot of Feast of Booths occurred in the fall. This created an opportunity to get away from the "ticket-for-an-event" language and root the "selling of tickets" in Jewish values and a community-building perspective. One congregation in Cleveland adopted this practice a couple of years ago and extended the following invitation to prospective members on its Web site:

We invite nonmembers to share the High Holy Day period with us, not as "ticket buyers," but as members of our congregation for the Hebrew month of Tishrei. For the same cost as "tickets," you will have seats at all High Holy Day Services, plus these invitations:

- Introduction to Judaism seminar
- Selichot service in a member's home
- Luncheon on the first day of Rosh Hashanah (extra cost and subject to availability)
- Age-appropriate High Holy Day educational programs for children
- Tashlich ceremony on first day of Rosh Hashanah
- Shabbat services and children's services
- Help erect our Sukkah
- Sukkot services in our Sukkah on Friday, including a potluck supper
- Simchat Torah celebration on Saturday morning, followed by a potluck lunch
- Kabbalat Shabbat services on Friday evening
- The September and October issues of our newsletter

Tishrei members will receive a detailed High Holy Days schedule and more information on these events. After enjoying the month of Tishrei with our community, if you join the Havurah before January 1, you can apply the full cost of your Tishrei Membership to your dues.[7]

I have heard from a few congregations that this approach has been the most energizing and successful in bringing a sense of sacred

purpose to this holiest time in the Jewish year. As one rabbinic colleague, who wishes to remain anonymous, wrote to me after insti-
tuting this idea, "Once people calling for tickets understand it, they
like it very much. Our ad begins, 'You can't buy a ticket to be part
of a community!'"

While not using Tishrei membership per se, other congregations are experimenting with alternative cost structures that appeal
more to *nadiv lev* (freewill offerings) of the heart. One example
comes from Congregation Beit Haverim in Atlanta courtesy of a
former president:

> At Bet Haverim in Atlanta, we have had an extremely successful High
> Holy Days appeal the past two years. Prior to that we charged non-
> members to attend, with the result that some were not coming out
> of inability to pay, and many of our members ended up policing the
> door, checking lists, taking checks, and so on. So we began an
> experiment last year, placing a donation card on each chair for all
> services and having a member of the executive committee or the rabbi
> make an appeal at each service. People could mail in the donation
> card after services. Last year we raised more than we had antici-
> pated from tickets. This year was even more successful. We specifi-
> cally broadened our appeal to include members, beginning with a
> 100 percent commitment from the board, rabbi, and cantor. For
> every hour of congregant time put into the appeal, we raised about
> $3,000, which is a good way to look at the success of any fund-
> raising activity.

The concept of dues or financial contribution for the upkeep of
one's community is an ancient concept in Jewish life. The expression of commitment to God, Torah, and the Jewish people through
the contribution of financial resources for a purpose greater than
one's own livelihood is profound. Whatever structure you participate in, money, viewed as a spiritual tool, is exchanged as a sign of
responsibility both to and from the faith community that we enter
into a sacred relationship with. It is a sign of covenant and commitment to each other's individual and collective welfare.

5

ORGANIZING MONEY

Capital Campaigns and Fund-Raising

Let them make Me a sanctuary that I may dwell among them.
—Exod. 25:8

No sooner had the Israelites left Egypt (in Hebrew, *Mitzrayim* or "narrow, constricted place") than the first major resource gathering campaign began in order to construct the Tent of Meeting. This holy space was located in the center of the Israelite camp for the many years of desert journeying and served as a spiritual center for the people as they were in transition from an oppressive and familiar life to an unknown land of promise and possibility. The Jewish people's movement from a slave *(eved)* mentality of scarcity and impoverishment to one of abundance and sacred service *(avodah,* sharing the same word root as *eved)* is reflected in the freehearted offerings that are used to build the *Mishkan* (sanctuary) for God and sacred service.

Granted, driven by fear and anxiety in Moses' absence while he was communing with God on Mount Sinai, the people had gathered resources not too long before to build a calf of gold. Seeing the danger expressed in the biblical story about turning the work of our hands into the very thing we idolized or are overly attached to, the later rabbinic commentators draw our attention to the fact that God asks for a dwelling place to be constructed for holy conversation and sacrifice "among the people," not in the physical structure per se (Exod. 25:8, as quoted above).

Fund-raising in congregations is ideally "soul-raising" and is viewed as a community-building activity. We are all willing to spend

63

money on things we value, such as education for our children, travel, art, culture, and so on. When it comes to organizing money in our faith communities, we can drift into collecting resources for our own "golden calves"—projects, edifices, or programs, enterprises that do not connect to our mission as communities. Yet, if we value our spiritual growth and home, we need to raise the money to provide salaries for our rabbis, teachers, and professionals, and to maintain or create buildings in which we can deepen our spiritual lives, teach our children, organize social action work, and develop warm, welcoming communities.[1]

I prefer the term "organizing money" to the traditional language of fund-raising, as it implies the resources already exist in the community and need to be organized according to the group's values and objectives. The term was coined by Jeffrey Dekro, president of the Shefa Fund, a nonprofit organization that helps individuals and other organizations direct their investments and *tzedakah* to issues and organizations in a Jewish values-based manner.[2] It reflects the concept that asking people for money is optimally about bringing them more deeply into communal relationship. We are not only asking people for contributions, we are organizing their involvement in a shared endeavor. This means, among other things, making sure the mission of our community and the goals for which we organize resources are clearly communicated to the membership. It means educating people about our religious traditions as part of fund-raising and seeing any solicitation or campaign as an educational opportunity. It means strengthening our relationships with our membership and their connection to the community as a whole.

It is important to openly connect the organization of funds to what inspires people about their community. Telling the history, accomplishments, and mission of your congregation as part of a capital campaign is one way of honoring the past while building for the future, and making sure that generations are linked in such a major endeavor. People do not generally give money to abstract concepts. They give because of meaningful relationships, shared values, and a sense that their story is connected in some way to the larger story of the project for which funds are being organized.

Historically, as Jews came to North America, especially in the late nineteenth century and through the Second World War, they sought to establish organizations and charitable funds to help newer immigrants and support the emerging Jewish community. By the

1940s and '50s, Jews began moving to the suburbs and, modeled after many of the suburban churches built during that time, raised funds to build synagogues in these newly developing areas as well. The proliferation of capital campaigns and the growth of synagogue movements, Jewish community centers, federations, and many other Jewish organizations in Canada and the United States led to intensified fund-raising, building, and expansion of professional staff from the 1950s and onwards.

While the outcome of organizing money for these endeavors has produced remarkable results in the solidification and development of the North American Jewish community, the process of raising funds has given rise anew to the age-old questions: How do we keep our focus on the connecting Source "among the people" and building sacred community, and not lose our focus in raising funds for their own sake? How is money organized and how might we keep our spiritual values front and center as we pursue the sacred task of aligning values with the resources we raise to manifest them?

CREATING THE OPPORTUNITY FOR A MITZVAH: ORGANIZING MONEY THROUGHOUT THE YEAR

Creating an opportunity for members of a community to share financial resources necessitates being clear on what money is being raised for, how it will be used, and how the fund-raising is connected to the values, mission, and strategic goals of the community.

To this end, I always encourage congregations, prior to or as part of a fund-raising activity or campaign, to spend time studying Jewish texts and traditions around money, such as those described in this book, or to go through a community-wide education process such as the one outlined in the sample lesson in the appendices. Clergy, educators, and other staff can be involved in fund-raising, avoiding potential conflicts of interest and honoring their own comfort level and ability, and can be central in keeping the religious values and the mission and goals of the faith community at the center of the fund-raising effort. There exists an opportunity for the rabbi to be an educator about Jewish approaches to money and community, even if she or he is uncomfortable or not prepared to be involved in asking for contributions.

Of course, it is not everyone's path to join a faith community and leap into raising money, nor should it be. However, everyone will need to think about what financial commitment he or she will

make as part of membership. Just as it is the goal of a congregation to provide multiple points of entry for members' involvement
in its programming, so too a community can aim to create multiple ways for its members (and sometimes nonmembers) to support the congregation's ongoing work in the area of organizing
money.

As I mentioned before, rabbis, teachers, and other staff can be
involved in ongoing consciousness raising and education about
money, values, and Jewish tradition in ways that are comfortable
for them (such as *divrei Torah* or "sermons," adult and child education classes, newsletter and Web site updates). Members can offer
inspiring written or oral testimonies about the transformative impact of belonging to their community, thus reminding members
of the history and mission of their community. Board or fund-raising committee members can make solicitation calls or hold fund-
raising events or activities tied to meaningful times in the Jewish or
civil calendar (High Holy Days, Thanksgiving, Pesach, lifecycle
events) and thereby increase the incentive to give and members'
understanding of what values and objectives contributions are
tied to.

As a general rule, synagogues do not meet their annual operating expenses by dues alone. In many communities, membership
dues account for 65 to 75 percent of operating costs. Many congregations, especially new ones, must rely on raising funds in addition
to membership dues to meet operating expenses. Annual fund-raising campaigns (often "kicked off" at the High Holy Days when
the majority of Jews attend synagogue services) and a variety of
fund-raising programs such as auctions, dinners, and cultural events,
are commonly held in most synagogues. *Scrip* has become an increasingly popular fund-raising tool. Members purchase coupons
for use at a variety of local stores, and a small percentage of the sales
are then given to the synagogue that sells the scrip. Even here, a
faith community can make a values-based statement by researching
the various employment, purchasing, and product manufacturing
practices of a particular store and supporting those that are in alignment with its values.

When creating events aimed at raising funds, honoring contributions of time and service is as important as acknowledging and
honoring financial gifts, and can often inspire greater giving as a
result. Even when honoring people, the organizers of the fund-raising effort can approach additional or already committed sponsors

to strengthen and build community while achieving budgetary goals. Campaign leaders might ask someone to underwrite the gift-recognition event, subsidize the cost of a ticket so it is more accessible to those with fewer means, or create challenge funds for a social justice cause that is tied to the event. Matching funds or "last money in," where someone agrees to match funds as they are raised or contribute an additional sum when a goal is reached, are ways to encourage maximal participation and ownership of the goals in a fund-raising endeavor.

One community spent time outlining the main Jewish values it wanted emphasized as part of any fund-raising effort and made the study and understanding of those values key to their training of their fund-raising team before solicitations began for their capital campaign. (See an example of such a list of values in the case study in chapter 7.) These Jewish values informed the way relationships would be built and funds solicited, as well as served as part of the educational material used in the solicitations and community-wide education in connection with the campaign.

CAPITAL CAMPAIGNS

In the realm of organizing money, building or refurbishing an existing building is often one of the defining moments in the life of a congregation. Through such an effort, the congregation can live out religious values, both in the process by which the funds are raised, as well as in the kind of structure built. It is important for the professional and lay leadership to help everyone feel like they are valued contributors and to remind people of the Jewish view that individuals are responsible for communal life. (See chapter 1 for examples.) Of course, what drives a successful building campaign is not only values, but a commitment to the mission and vision of the congregation or organization as it is translated into the programming and religious life of the new structure. Values are crucial to "how" money will be reused and allocated, but "what" will take place in the new building is even more critical for uniting a community around a campaign.

One example of organizing money for a building project and simultaneously strengthening community aligned with Jewish values is from the Jewish Reconstructionist Congregation of Evanston, Illinois. In their precampaign phase, they laid out the values-based foundation for the fund-raising as follows:

We believe that a congregation's building and its programs are not ends in themselves, but rather serve as a means to a much greater end—the ongoing creation of sacred community. . . . In a capital campaign, this will be our guiding principle.

Jewish tradition has long considered fund-raising to be an important and sacred aspect of communal life. . . . Our campaign will be an important and necessary achievement for our congregation, because the entire process—from fund-raising design to construction—will be carried out according to our deeply held core Jewish values.

In a formal campaign and design process, we will keep the congregation informed, seeking out and listening to feedback from every JRC member, and making sure we maintain our full range of programs. All committees will be asked for their comments. Open information meetings, focus groups, and avenues for written feedback will be extended to the membership at large.

In the end, we intend this effort to strengthen the very fabric of our community. We will seek 100 percent participation in our campaign not simply because of the financial benefits we may reap, but because we want our members to feel truly invested in their congregation. The most successful fund-raising campaigns seek not simply to raise capital, but to strengthen members' commitment to one another and to their collective future.[3]

The JRC process and document address the need for a compelling vision or "case statement" for financial support. Every community has different building needs and uses different approaches to meet those needs. A case statement might address questions such as: What Jewish values of community do you want your building to embody? What type of capital campaign and resulting physical structure will best support the creation of community?

An outside consultant, a professional from a national movement or federation office, or other congregations who have been through a values-based capital campaign, can help you avoid wasted time and burnout. Even here, be up front and ask the prospective consultant whether they will also focus on values and building the community, not only the building itself in the course of a capital campaign. You may need to bring in a consultant or movement professional to help revitalize a capital campaign that will include multiple phases over a number of years. As in the initial stages of a capital campaign, leaders will need to ensure Jewish values and a clear programmatic vision coming from the mission of the community are central, and may need to frequently remind members why their participation is a crucial part of building a "sacred dwelling place." As well, leaders will want to contact other congregations or organizations that have done values-based and capital campaigns.

It is equally important to interview architects using similar criteria as for a consultant, including concerns about energy, environmental impact, efficiency, and religious aesthetics. Once an architect is engaged and plans begin to unfold, make the vision concrete with drawings, models, newsletter, and Web site updates to keep people involved in their campaign as a community-building activity.

The standard wisdom in fund-raising ventures such as capital campaigns is that 80 percent of the funds will come from 20 percent of the givers. In faith communities we strive for a broader support base, and even a 100 percent participation goal is not too lofty as long as a variety of opportunities are provided for members to give. This still does not necessarily mean that 80 percent of the funds will *not* come from 20 percent of the donors. Still, campaign planners should keep in mind that maximizing participation is based on a Jewish value (remember the biblical concepts of "half-shekel" and *nadiv lev*!) and offers an opportunity to build community. One way to broaden the opportunities for members to contribute is to have a number of fund-raising events that vary in cost and that allow people to participate according to their capacity. Another way of demonstrating commitment to the capital campaign is to ask campaign solicitors to make their own gift first. Contributions may take the form of gifts or future bequests from planned giving.

Regardless of your participation goals, it is still important to know who your larger givers will be over three to five years and how many $10,000, $25,000, $50,000, or higher gifts you can count on in an initial quiet phase before the campaign is fully launched. This helps avoid launching an unrealistic capital campaign or drawing one out over more than three to five years, after which the energy and enthusiasm can begin to wane and initial cost projections can escalate. Without this planning, a capital campaign can undermine a sense of community instead of strengthening it.

Preparing a case statement or special brochure about your community that shows your larger place and impact on your city can help raise funds beyond your own constituents. Havurah Shalom in Portland, Oregon, raised thousands of dollars from outside individuals and organizations towards their reclamation of a downtown warehouse. The shared commitment towards the revitalization of the downtown core and the life of the city inspired the gifts from outside their membership base and denominational group.

How contributions are acknowledged is another key area of organizing money in a capital campaign that concretely demonstrates values. This is especially important to clarify before launching a campaign and creating expectations or operating on assumptions that will result in conflict and misunderstanding later on. (Planners might ask, for example, "Will donations be acknowledged equally in a location in the building, or will naming opportunities be made available? Or will there be areas where no donor recognition is allowed?") The Jewish concern around money, power, and status as it relates to the reasons one builds a sacred space and how one is acknowledged is expressed in this text from the Middle Ages by Yehudah HaChasid:

> He who builds a monument for his own glory will not be remembered. There once was a man who built a magnificent synagogue. The community wanted to contribute money toward the construction in order to participate in the "mitzvah," but the man refused to accept any outside help because he wanted this synagogue to be a memorial solely for himself and his offspring. His dynasty came to an end.[4]

Dan Hotchkiss, in his book *Ministry and Money,* makes the following observation:

> Synagogues have generally been . . . more willing to recognize large givers by encouraging them to announce their gifts, and by affixing plaques and naming buildings for them. . . . An increasing number of congregations have now begun to question traditional ways of funding the congregation. . . . Discomfort about inequality of wealth is a part of American culture that touches every faith community.[5]

Acknowledging gifts and honoring each other in community is certainly not antithetical to Jewish ethics or practice. Many communities and organizations have walls or plaques of recognition that may feature lists of names by giving category, or "trees of life" with branches and leaves containing the names of contributors. Other choices around acknowledgment include whether names will be listed in a hierarchy of giving or just alphabetically, whether recognition plaques or "leafs" will vary in size according to gifts or will all be equal in size; whether rooms, seats, ritual items in the sanctuary, or only certain areas or items can be sponsored but not designated with a recognition plaque. What I am advocating for here is that campaign leaders include a process for making such decisions as part of the capital campaign and recognize what any of these choices will mean to current and future members.

Oseh Shalom, a congregation in Laurel, Maryland, decided that all of its acknowledgment plaques would be of equal size and located in columns outside the sanctuary. No recognition plaques would be allowed in the sanctuary itself. The congregation had the sanctuary roof designed with a dome formed from a series of concentric rings. The entire community was invited to work with their rabbi and educators to explore passages from the Torah in small study groups and to suggest excerpts that they wished to be affixed to the concrete rings in the dome. Households were then able to make further contributions to the capital campaign by sponsoring a letter or a word from the chosen passage. Not all the rings were filled by chosen passages, leaving room for future generations to continue the study. This successful educational and spiritual exercise enhanced the capital campaign and strengthened the bonds of the members to each other, the mission of their community, Torah, and Jewish values of study and participatory decision making.

Another example of organizing a capital campaign to reflect the spiritual mission of a faith community comes from Congregation Beth Israel in Media, Pennsylvania. At CBI, *tikkun olam* (social action) has always been a significant part of the fabric of their community. In 1997, when launching their building campaign, members spoke up and suggested that they extend the blessings they were fortunate to experience in building their own sanctuary by building a home for those who were homeless or could not afford to purchase one. Under the leadership of Rabbi Linda Potemken, the community discussed the issue in its religious action, education, capital campaign, and executive committees, and an ad hoc committee was formed to come up with a plan.

What emerged was *bateam,* based on the Hebrew word for "houses" but spelled intentionally in English to include the word "team." Campaign organizers made a commitment to dedicate 3 percent of every capital campaign contribution towards low-income housing construction. Their work was inspired by Leviticus 19:9-10: "When you reap the harvest of your land, you shall not reap to

the edges of your field, or gather the gleanings of your harvest....
You shall leave them for the poor and the stranger."

The congregation partnered with a local civic community-im-
provement project that was seeking to revitalize the city through
housing rehabilitation, new construction, and mortgage counseling. When the congregation had raised the cost of a complete home,
the congregation was notified and a home was dedicated to sym-
bolize Beth Israel's achievement. Members of the congregation were
also given the opportunity to volunteer with the agency to help
clear debris, landscape, or perform nonskilled construction tasks.
This is a wonderful example of building community internally as
well as reaching out through one's own capital campaign to build
relationships across faith communities, government, and the public
at large, all while living out one's own communal mission and connecting to ancient religious values.

God is in the details, as the saying goes, manifest in each decision we make individually and as a community. Once the building
is built, the challenge to live out our values in godly action continues. The Shulchan Aruch, a sixteenth-century compendium of
halakhah ("Jewish law" or literally "path" or "way") suggests that
people should not act irreverently in synagogues or in schools of
Torah, that they may not conduct business in these buildings,
unless it is mitzvah business, such as budgeting *tzedakah* funds.
If a person has come into these buildings for purely personal
reasons, as for example to locate someone, they should read over
some Written Torah text or recite some selection of Oral Torah
(Talmud) as they try to find the person, so that it will not appear
that they entered just for their own purposes. And if they don't
know how to study, they should say to one of the children, "Read
me the verses you are studying." Or let them stay for a while
and then go, because the very act of sitting in these buildings is
a mitzvah.[6]

Once the doors are opened, the opportunity and challenge to
keep our values and sense of sacred community continues. One
congregation I have worked with that had a very successful building campaign wanted to know how much to pay its caretaking staff
as the building was going up. They discovered in their research of
local faith communities across the religious spectrum that none of
them was paying their caretaking staff the recommended living wage
in their area. (Neither were many other for-profit or nonprofit organizations.) The leaders and members reflected deeply on their own

value of *tzedek* (justice) and determined that it compelled the synagogue to pay the living wage, and to speak out in public discussions about fair wages.

There are times when we as faith communities will feel compelled to make values-based choices in financial matters that will be controversial. In fact, it is in the realm of money and values that our values, identities, and faith can be most severely tested and most inspirationally lived out. A capital campaign is a profound opportunity to build community, not just build a building, and to help people articulate why they are part of the community to begin with.

WRESTLING WITH THE ANGEL: ETHICS AND ORGANIZING MONEY

Just as the Hebrew Bible depicts Jacob wrestling with an angel (Gen. 32) to extract a blessing and live into the potential of "Israel" (as Jacob is renamed), a faith-based community wrestles with ethical considerations and dilemmas in the financial arena that can define a community's life. Wrestling with our ethics may mean we leave the encounter with the blessings of both clarified values and deepened faith. It may also mean slower and more thoughtful decision making that frustrates quick action and easy solutions but results in decisions more connected to a godly purpose.

In one recent discussion within the modern orthodox Jewish community, Rabbi Daniel Feldman states:

> Although it is part of the job of the *Gabbai Tzedakah* [head of fund-raising] to be persuasive . . . Jewish law places the responsibility on the *Gabbai Tzedakah* not to try and exact a donation that is beyond the means of the donor, who acquiesces only to avoid embarrassment. Humiliation is an inappropriate tactic even when an individual is capable of larger donations, and thus negotiations in that area must be done privately. The great merit associated with one who persuades another to be generous is applicable only when the donor is capable of such generosity.[7]

This perspective asks us to see that process and outcome, the form and content of our fund-raising activities, are inseparable, even when we collect money for objectives that are themselves just and charitable. Cost and benefit are not only economic terms but spiritual measurements. What are the consequences to our own souls if we raise the funds we need but rupture relationships, alienate others, and leave the impression that the goals of a faith-based community justify the means? This does not mean the ethics of organizing money prohibit inviting people to stretch in their giving or perhaps challenging an individual's or group's priorities and spending patterns. It does mean we avoid splitting actions in the financial realm from religious values and practice.

Rabbi Feldman goes on to relate the need to be transparent and honest in representing the fundraising to one's own community and any external organization being asked for funds:

> The *Gabbai Tzedakah* is asked to be honest not only in dealing with the finances but also in their methodology of raising them. Similarly the organization must be absolutely honest in representing itself to the government in reference to aid that the government provides, and not to attempt to extract more funds than are deserved, which is also considered theft. It should be emphasized that the *halakhah* adds its endorsement to the tenets of secular law in these matters, whose restrictions become automatic points of *halakhah* as well (*dina d'malchutah dina* or "honoring the laws of the country").[8]

I find these assertions, based on Jewish tradition, a reminder that our actions, especially in financial matters, have impact in so many areas of our lives. They also reflect the idea that Jewish values are to guide our behavior not only in our relationships with the Jewish community itself but are directions for our actions across religious and political lines. The religious principle articulated above can apply to any community or organization.

There is another *halakhik* principle—a *mitzvah ha-ba'ah b'aveirah* (mitzvah affirmed through a transgression)—that will provide a tool for judging ethically difficult situations. In the Talmud, we learn that a stolen *lulav* (palm branch) may not be used to fulfill the mitzvah of *lulav* on the holiday of Sukkot, the eight-day Festival of Booths and Ingathering that occurs in the fall. The Talmud answers that whatever the value of fulfilling the mitzvah, the tainted means of fulfillment (in this case, the *lulav*) renders the mitzvah invalid. The ends do not justify the means. In another part of the Talmud, the sages state:

> The Rabbis taught: If a man steals a beam and builds it into a palace, Beth Shammai says that one must demolish the whole palace and

restore the beam to its owner. Beth Hillel, however, says that the latter can claim only the money value of the beam, so as not to place obstacles in the way of penitents. (Babylonian Talmud, *Gittin* 55a)

While the Talmudic Sages generally favored Hillel's views over Shammai's, the text above does raise the question: should the community accept contributions of questionable funds? The question the Talmudic text asks of us today is whether the principles articulated above should be extended to contributions of funds acquired in business activities that are not illegal but, Jewishly considered, unethical.

Take, for instance, the debate over whether to accept the philanthropic contributions of individuals who have become wealthy through the sale of addictive or harmful substances, and whether, even if we accept such contributions, we should honor the donors. Should faith communities or religious organizations refuse donations from those who have made their money in ways that the community considers morally unacceptable? How should a faith community or religious organization respond if it is offered a large gift from an individual who earns his fortune from morally difficult products or services? What if the source of the funds is a company known to be a major polluter, a company that fails to treat its workers ethically, or a company that disregards the well-being of the community in which it is located? What is morally or Jewishly appropriate in each case? What do you imagine would be the practical consequence over time if the community began making moral judgments about our donors and the provenance of their gifts? Has an issue of this kind ever arisen in your organization? What was your organization's response? Was it ethically appropriate? What if you built a building or raised funds for operating expenses and later found out the donor was involved in racist or other social or environmentally destructive actions? If a donor's gift was attached to a naming opportunity in your building, would you remove the donor's name? If you did, would you also return the money?

I have seen responses on both sides of the issue, from not accepting any contributions from individuals or organizations that have questionable moral and ethical track records, to taking any funds for a cause that will have positive effect and forward godly action on the planet. The outcome, as the Torah states, is not so far across the sea, nor way up in heaven, but in our own hands and hearts. It is advisable to tackle such questions when you are not under pressure to make a decision about a specific gift, and to develop values-based policies that will inform the community's response to such a situation.

Rabbi Arthur Waskow, author of *Down to Earth Judaism,* also raises important questions in his chapter on money about the ethical questions communities might also ask, even when there is no problem with the way funds have been raised. Rabbi Waskow, pointing out that congregations, religious organizations, or cultural centers are not only a collection of people, but also of resources asks, "Should the board of each one . . . offer ceramic cups for wine or coffee instead of paper and plastic? Should the synagogue bookstore/gift shop offer energy-saving light bulbs and water saving shower heads for sale as sacred objects alongside prayer shawls?"[9] Responding to these and a whole set of questions about ethics and money from a faith perspective means not only to assess what financial resources we will accept, but also how we hold ourselves to similar standards of socioeconomic, values-based consciousness in how we spend the money we organize.

LAST THOUGHTS

I remember an interaction with a president of a congregation at one of the money and Jewish values seminars I was leading. The participant had come to the workshop with a great deal of anxiety about her role leading a fund-raising effort directed at hiring a part-time rabbi. As the workshop progressed and we studied Jewish texts about money and building sacred community across the centuries, she leapt up enthusiastically at one point and said, "I get it now! I am not asking people for money. I am creating an opportunity for them to fulfill a mitzvah—to use their financial resources towards a holy end and to help build this community!" On returning home she brought her enthusiasm back to her board, convinced that the prevailing attitude they were operating under in proposing a part-time rabbinic position was underestimating what the community could raise if they approached their campaign from the position that they were creating opportunities for giving and building holy community. Persuaded by their president's newfound passion, the board agreed to a two-thirds rabbinic position and a subsequent campaign that exceeded expectations.

The desire to give of one's self runs deep in the human soul. All too often, fear and the absence of open communication, along with unclear goals and lack of an explicit connection to Jewish values and approaches that emphasize holiness and vision, not actual capacity and willingness to share resources, can inhibit organizing money in communities of faith.

Judaism does not split the religious from the business or financial end of a faith community's ongoing life. Such a split often leads those who are searching for spiritual answers to the challenges of contemporary life to cynicism with organized religious communities. When done right, however, fund-raising can be a powerful spiritual, healing, and inspiring exercise in fulfilling our potential as sacred communities and as individuals seeking to live out our values in concrete action that will have impact long after we are gone.

6

TZEDAKAH

Justice Through Giving

And if your brother becomes poor and his means fail him with
you, then you will strengthen him, be he a stranger
or a settler, he shall live with you.

—Lev. 25:35

Even a poor person who is kept alive by tzedakah funds
must give tzedakah from what they receive.

—Shulchan Aruch, Yoreh Deah 251:12

As the texts above demonstrate, and as we discussed in chapter 1,
the importance of supporting those with fewer resources is woven
throughout millennia of Jewish religious civilization. Caring for those
that are in need has been traditionally seen as a way of doing godly
work in the world and mirroring Divine compassion. *Tzedakah* (giving with justice and compassion) has been a foundational element of
Jewish communal life since its earliest stages and has come to be
understood in contemporary practice as giving over and above general costs such as dues or capital campaigns.

Tzedakah is an area in which many congregations have well-
developed programs and can provide leadership. Generally, tzedakah
collection on a communal level is done by gathering funds and pass-
ing them on to other constituencies or individuals within one's congregation, to other groups or organizations within one's larger faith
community, as well as to causes and groups outside of one's religious or denominational lines, whether locally or globally. In fact,

from the Hebrew Bible to contemporary Jewish life, collecting and giving tzedakah is viewed as an expression of justice or just action in the world. To practice justice when making financial or other resources available to those in need, we must view the world from a larger perspective, one in which borders disappear. From a Jewish perspective, the interdependence and vulnerability of the world we live in is the lens through which we are asked to view our stewardship of the resources we have been blessed with.

The very root of the word tzedakah, *tzedek* (justice), has historically informed the giving and distribution of funds by Jews, whether individually or collectively. The Hebrew vocabulary does not include a word that can be translated as "charity." The reason for this is at the very heart of the Jewish concept of economic justice. The Hebrew Bible views God as the source of all creation (see Gen. 1) and human beings as stewards of all that preceded them. From this perspective, human beings are committed to equitably share what God has bestowed to them, and this sharing is designated in Hebrew as tzedakah.[1]

Tzedakah is not intended to be an unfeeling act or disconnected from passion for a just cause, but feelings in and of themselves should not dictate our willingness to give. While love is expressed in the generous sharing of resources and is seen as reflecting God's love and concern for all beings, the giving of tzedakah is not viewed as an act that is required or determined by the depth or even presence of good feelings towards another. Rather it is seen as stemming from a sense of justice and equity. We have responsibility and obligation to give tzedakah whether we feel like giving or not. The Sages in the Talmud promote an activist stance by underscoring the many references in the Hebrew Bible to the pursuit of justice. The implication here is that while we may intellectually endorse concepts such as justice and giving to those who need, we must not sit back and congratulate ourselves for holding such ideals. Rather, we must actively enshrine them in our individual and communal actions. The Hebrew prophets were particularly vocal about challenging the status quo. Their passion for protecting those in need and challenging the idea that a religious life could be separated from economic and social justice influenced the rabbis of the Talmudic and later ages to develop substantive directives around tzedakah:

> Tzedakah is not an aspiration but a legal requirement. Every person, including the poor, is required by Jewish law to fulfill this

duty. The codes of Jewish law specify an absolute minimal contribution level, a median level, an upper level in terms of specific amounts and percentages of income. . . . Tzedakah refers to a duty to be performed whether or not one can or does love the recipient.[2]

Rabbi Toba Spitzer of Newton, Massachusetts, who has led congregations in the study of money and Jewish values and written extensively on this issue, points out that the mitzvah of tzedakah is a natural extension of the Jewish people's covenant with God. Though not referred to systemically as tzedakah in the Hebrew Bible, the covenantal understanding is reflected in a series of directives around giving to the community at large and supporting the vulnerable in society:

> The covenantal approach to poverty and the poor has powerful implications for consideration of these issues today. The first lesson is that the production of wealth is conditional and contingent upon the just treatment of the less powerful in society, from those without the means to support themselves to the laborers one hires. The creation of community, of society, is inherently a sacred act, and so all aspects of it must be regulated with God's intent in mind. The source of the sustenance of the community is ultimately the Holy One, and so God's justice must be an integral component of the production and distribution of that sustenance.[3]

It is worth noting that in the conversion process to Judaism, as it began to be structured postbiblically, in the rabbinic times of the Talmud, the first *mitzvot* that the sages said should be taught to the proselyte were the essential areas of caring economically for those in need.[4] Along with a number of *halakhik* (legal categories) and *mitzvot* outlined in the Mishnah, Talmud, and later commentaries, many homiletical stories illustrate the Jewish values beneath the *mitzvot* on tzedakah:

> Once Rabbi Samson of Shepetivka, went to see Rabbi Ezekiel Landau, the great sage and chief rabbi of Prague, to discuss matters of scholarship. The two rabbis had never met before. Rabbi Samson approached Rabbi Ezekiel in disguise, dressed as a beggar, asking for alms. Rabbi Ezekiel, who was a very busy man, treated Rabbi Samson very rudely, whereupon Rabbi Samson said,

"How can you, a sage and a religious leader, treat a poor person in this fashion? You should rise at my presence, and you should respond to my needs, for God's Presence stands at my side. As it is written: God stands at the right hand of the needy to save him from those who would condemn him." (Ps. 109:31)[5]

In fact, members of the community were encouraged to offer tzedakah at the first signs of another member's financial difficulty to try to prevent a further decline in economic status.[6] The Sages also argued that indifference to the welfare of those closest to us could not be separated from the ethical practices of tzedakah in the larger world. Recognizing that it is often easier to be motivated to give to causes in the community, the thirteenth-century *Hasidei Ashkenaz* (German pietist) Rabbi Yehudah HeChasid wrote:

A rich man used to donate money to the community's "tzedakah" fund and ask the administrator to distribute it to the poor. Now this rich man had an impoverished brother; in fact, all of his relatives were destitute. The rabbi told the rich man, "The money you dole out to the poor through the 'tzedakah' fund is not 'tzedakah.' Rather, it causes tze'akah, 'sobbing' by your relatives. It is far better that you give these funds to your needy brother and penniless relatives."[7]

I find the social-spiritual experiment of the Hasidei Ashkenaz in thirteenth- and fourteenth-century Germany quite fascinating, as in many ways they parallel some of the Christian ascetic trends of the time, but without the monastic element. Living out the tension between *devekut* (cleaving to God) in one's own soul and living as full partners in community provided a difficult challenge to the adherents and to the non-Hasidic members of the communities in which they coexisted. In the realm of tzedakah the Hasidei Ashkenaz's desire to move beyond the "letter of the law" led to other teachings on the mitzvah of tzedakah. Rabbi Yehudah goes on in another section of *Sefer Hasidim* (The Book of the Pietists):

A man who was the most astute buyer of merchandise in town devoted all his spare time to Torah study. One day, a widow asked him to buy a certain article for her. He declined, saying, "I'm sorry, but I simply cannot give up my Torah studies." A venerable old rabbi interjected, "Do you think that you are better than Rabbi

Gamliel and Rabbi Yehoshua? The Talmud tells us that they inter-
rupted their Torah studies to go to the market to buy an animal
for the wedding feast of Rabbi Gamliel's son (Babylonian Talmud,
Makkot 14a), and on the way discussed Torah topics. You should
do the same. When you buy the article for the widow, keep your
mind on Torah issues. And when you buy merchandise at a favor-
able price, the money you save her is counted as your "tzedakah,"
and God will repay you for your trouble.[8]

In the social justice system of giving in Jewish life and law, both
giver and receiver are seen as partners in living out godly action in
the world. Circumstances and roles may change in an instant, but
the commitment to the mitzvah of tzedakah goes unchanged. The
founder of modern Hasidism, the Baal Shem Tov, articulates the
partnership idea of tzedakah, where both the giver and receiver are
involved in actualizing the Divine attribute of compassion:

> When a rich person gives "tzedakah" they do a "mitzvah" . . . but
> when a poor person accepts "tzedakah," at first glance it seems
> that they are not doing a "mitzvah." But if the poor person re-
> ceives it with "kavannah" [or "heartfelt intention giving merit to
> the giver"] . . . then they are doing a mitzvah.[9]

Although tzedakah is rooted in the principle of justice, Judaism does
embrace the concept of giving out of love and kindness. Tzedakah is
required of all, and *gemilut hasadim* (acts of loving-kindness) are
available to everyone. *Gemilut hasadim* is love in action, generosity
towards all of creation, not only human beings, and the extension of
kindness and caring support for emotional, intellectual, and spiritual needs. This Jewish value and concept weaves its way through
the acts of tzedakah, binding together heart and hands. The sages of
the Talmud even elevated *gemilut hasadim* to a higher moral plane
than tzedakah: "One who gives a coin to a poor person is rewarded
with six blessings, but one who encourages that person with words
is rewarded with seven" (Babylonian Talmud, *Baba Batra* 9b).

The attitude that giving is about providing not only financial
"charity," but emotional, psychological, and spiritual support goes
back to the biblical texts on leaving gleanings of the fields for the
stranger and the home-born. Tzedakah and *gemilut hasadim* are
ways the whole of the community holds up those in temporary or
long-term need. In classical Jewish sources, poverty was seen as a

social misfortune rather than as a Divine punishment.[10] Neither the poor nor the potentially poor are ever dealt with generically. Jewish sources tend not to deal with "the poor" but focus on the individual (the widow, the orphan, the sojourner, and so forth).[11] Whether it be the Sabbath or the Jewish holy days and festivals, both biblical and rabbinic sources always made a connection with the experience of Israelite oppression in slavery and the need to empathize with any individual or group that has been made "other" or left behind by life circumstance. The sensitivities at play in the stewarding of one's God-given resources and—when one is in need, receiving of these resources—is given much attention in the act of tzedakah.

The Sages of the Talmud go as far as to state, "Better no giving at all than giving that humiliates" (Babylonian Talmud, *Hagigah* 5a). In other words, giving that comes with stereotyping, judgment, or condescension towards a group, or that undermines the recipient's sense of self, is seen as equally, if not more destructive than, allowing someone to suffer due to lack of material resources. In fact, to this day, discussions about tzedakah in the Jewish community often use the levels of tzedakah as outlined by the famous medieval commentator Maimonides as a benchmark for approaches to giving. As you read through his degrees of tzedakah (which I have rendered in inclusive language), consider the following questions as a community or as leadership of your faith community:

- How do we best provide for individuals who have fallen into need, remembering to protect their dignity even as we recognize their current indignity?
- What is the moral logic behind Maimonides's conception?
- How does his hierarchy compare with your community's methods and priorities?
- How useful are Maimonides's principles today? Do we need to find different approaches? If so, what needs to change?

There are eight degrees of tzedakah, one higher than the other:

The highest degree, exceeded by none, is that of the person who assists a poor person by providing them with a gift or a loan or by accepting them into a business partnership or by helping them find employment—in a word, by putting them where they can dispense with other people's aid. With reference to such aid, it is said, "You shall strengthen him, be he a stranger or a settler, he shall live with you" (Lev. 25:35), which means strengthen them in such manner that their falling into want is prevented.

A step below this stands the one who gives alms to the needy in such a manner that the giver knows not to whom he gives and the recipient knows not from whom it is that he takes. Such exemplifies performing the meritorious act for its own sake. An illustration would be the Hall of Secrecy in the ancient sanctuary where the righteous would place their gift clandestinely and where poor people of high lineage would come and secretly help themselves to succor.

The rank next to this is of those who drop money in the charity box. One should not drop money in the charity box unless one is sure that the person in charge is trustworthy, wise, and competent to handle the funds properly, as was Rabbi Hananya ben Teradyon.

One step lower is that in which the giver knows to whom they give but the poor person knows not from whom they receive. Examples of this were the great sages who would go forth and throw coins covertly into poor people's doorways. This method becomes fitting and exalted, should it happen that those in charge of the charity fund do not conduct its affairs properly.

A step lower is that in which the poor person knows from whom they are taking but the giver knows not to whom they are giving. Examples of this were the great sages who would tie their coins in their scarves, which they would fling over their shoulders so that the poor might help themselves without suffering shame.

The next degree lower is that of those who, with their own hand, bestow a gift before the poor person asks.

The next degree lower is that of those who give only after the poor person asks.

The next degree lower is that of those who give less than is fitting but gives graciously.

The next degree lower is that of those who gives morosely.[12]

While ultimately your answers to the questions posed before the Rambam's list may or may not align themselves with the degrees as he outlines them, the intentionality and thoughtfulness he invites us into is profound. He challenges us to move beyond "feel-good" giving that, while it does meet the criteria of tzedakah on a basic level, may create long-term dependencies or unintended psychospiritual consequences. Maimonides also raises the role of justice, as well as our motivations, in our acts of giving. His intent is not to stifle giving or ground us down in an internal debate about the purity of our motives. Rather, for the sake of justice and equity in the world, we are invited to audit our patterns of giving and see them as a direct expression of God's presence in the world. In the words of the Sages of the Talmud, "He who gives a coin to a poor man merits seeing the Divine Presence" (Babylonian Talmud, *Bava Batra* 10a).

Moses pleads with God on Mt. Sinai to behold the Divine presence. The Sages ask us to see giving as taking a step onto holy ground—where values and actions meet and we can glimpse the essence of the world as it can be. Giving itself becomes the very route for us to behold the same Presence that Moses experienced on the height of Sinai. We encounter that Presence in the daily activities of life at the foot of the mountain where we spend most of our lives.

CONTEMPORARY RESPONSES

While tzedakah is still a concept that holds meaning for many in the Jewish community, it is often the overall idea, rather than the underlying textual and philosophical basis for tzedakah, with which most Jews are familiar. Education about the texts and principles underlying tzedakah can be empowering for individuals and their community and have a powerful effect on the understanding of and motivation for giving. Bob Barkin, a member of congregation Adat Shalom in Bethesda, Maryland, wrote the following in a *dvar Torah* he gave at his congregation after attending a workshop on money and Jewish values I led there. Notice the connection Bob makes to one of the core Jewish texts we studied in chapter 1 and the alignment of values and actions:

> The first lesson I learned is that tzedakah is as central to Judaism as the Shema itself [Hear Israel, YHWH is our God, God is one]. When we say the Shema, we include the phrase *b'chol l'vavkha, uv'khol nafshekha uv'khol me'odekha,* which our *siddur* [prayer book] translates as loving God "with all of your heart, with all of your soul and with all you have." The earliest understanding of this phrase directly ties *me'od* to your material wealth.

I think that check-writing should be the end point of an evaluation of our values. We need to identify those things that are most important to us and make the act of tzedakah an affirmative statement about those values.

When a connection is made—when a donor's values meet those values of a worthy cause—I believe there is a spark, a holy spark that empowers both the organization receiving and the person giving. This is the power of tzedakah.[13]

In Barkin's comments, directed towards fund-raising itself as a mechanism for tzedakah, the language of Jewish values replaces the traditional language of *mitzvot* (commandments). These are not mutually exclusive vocabularies. Jewish values are interwoven and inculcated in the daily acts of religious life and spiritual practice. For instance, it is a longstanding Jewish custom to give tzedakah at life-cycle and year-cycle events, before Shabbat, and at practically any communal function. Below are ideas for giving opportunities for throughout the Jewish year as imagined by the Shefa Fund of Philadelphia. Their list, which I have modified, includes some contemporary causes and concerns that might be recipients of giving, as well as educational and consciousness-raising opportunities.

Rosh Hashanah (The New Year)

The High Holy Day cycle is traditionally observed with *teshuvah, tzedakah,* and *tefillah* (repentance, sharing of wealth, and prayer). Rosh Hashanah, the New Year for the earth, is a time to direct tzedakah towards artistic projects that enlarge our sense of awe and connection.

Yom Kippur (The Day of Atonement)

For Yom Kippur, a day on which it is traditional to fast, many synagogues organize hunger-relief food drives. It's a good time to direct tzedakah toward organizations dedicated to eliminating poverty and achieving economic justice.

Sukkot/Shemini Atzeret (The Feast of Booths and the Eighth Day Festival)

During Sukkot, it is traditional to eat and sleep in a *sukkah* (temporary booth), which is open to the elements. For this reason, your community might want to focus its tzedakah work towards remind-ing us of our vulnerability within the natural world (such as ending homelessness).

SIMCHAT TORAH (CELEBRATION OF THE TORAH CYCLE)

The High Holy Days end with this "rejoicing of the Torah," tradi-tionally observed with all-night Torah readings. Tzedakah for edu-cation fits the spirit.

HANUKKAH

Hanukkah is an opportunity to link gift-giving with tzedakah in keep-ing with holiday themes: self-determination, religious freedom, and free speech.

TU B'SHEVAT (THE FIFTEENTH OF THE MONTH OF SHEVAT)

This "New Year of the Trees" is ripe for tzedakah dedicated to envi-ronmental preservation in the United States and Israel—and to eco-nomic justice for farmworkers and others in food industries.

PURIM

This Jewish holiday, in which we celebrate our identities, points us towards causes that support inclusion. Some suggestions for orga-nizations include: feminist causes, organizations that work against homophobia, those which support people with disabilities, multicultural families, and so forth.

PASSOVER

Passover expresses Jewish longings for freedom and a world in which our deepest values can be redeemed. Tzedakah dedicated to cam-paigns against slavery and human trafficking and to just treatment for immigrants and "strangers" is appropriate for this remembrance of the Exodus.

YOM HASHOAH

In response to the incalculable loss of Jewish life in the Holocaust, which Yom HaShoah commemorates, tzedakah might best be devoted to the rebuilding of Jewish life and culture and to organizing against anti-Semitism, racism, and neo-fascism.

YOM HAATZMAUT

Celebrate Israel's day of independence with tzedakah devoted to peace and security in the Middle East.

SHAVUOT (THE FESTIVAL OF WEEKS)

Shavuot celebrates the covenant made at Mt. Sinai, where every Jew who joined the Exodus from Egypt, as well as "the souls of all future generation" (Talmud), were given the Torah as revelation about how to live our lives. Tzedakah on this day might be devoted to projects of generational continuity and to legal activism for corporate, government, and judicial responsibility.

TISHA B'AV (THE NINTH OF THE MONTH OF AV)

This fast day recalls the destruction of both of Jerusalem's temples by outside forces intent on obliterating the Jewish people. *Tisha B'Av* also marks the birth of the messianic hope for redemption. Tzedakah for world peace, disarmament, and the eradication of genocidal weapons fulfills the spirit of *Tisha B'Av*.

TZEDAKAH FAIRS

Besides year-cycle and life-cycle opportunities to give tzedakah, there are many other programmatic and educational possibilities a faith community can explore. While youth and adult education classes on money, tzedakah, and Jewish values are certainly optimal, many congregations continue to develop innovative programming as a way of educating and motivating their membership to give more freely and fully to tzedakah. "Tzedakah fairs," for example, have increasingly been used as such a program opportunity for intergenerational learning. Some communities begin with one common activity, such as a discussion about tzedakah in general, and then people are divided generally based on the age of their children and go in groups to each of four stations for a 15- to 30-minute program, depending on the overall length of the event.

Each station involves a different kind of learning adjusted to meet the needs of the learners, from adolescents prior to bar or bat mitzvah to adults. Generally stations would include (1) text study and story-telling station; (2) an arts-based project, such as making family tzedakah boxes; (3) an activity station with perhaps a game involving Rambam's degrees of tzedakah or a play; (4) a prayer station where participants learn songs and prayers that teach us about tzedakah. The program would conclude with the entire group gathering to share what they learned or make decisions about where collected tzedakah would be designated.

Another exercise, called "hassle lines," requires leaders and participants, a large enough space, and those who can deal with lots of noise. Participants form two lines, facing each other, so everyone has a partner. One line is the "givers," and one is the "recipients." The leader gives the participants one of the scenarios from Rambam's ladder of tzedakah (discussed earlier in this chapter). For example, when the recipient asks for money, the giver offers a gift but is really grumpy.

Have each pair act out the assigned level of giving for at least one minute. (This is the noisy part: everyone plays his or her role simultaneously.) Then the leader stops the group and asks them how it felt to be the giver, how it felt to be the recipient, and how they wish the scene would have been different. Groups can do several of the rungs on the ladder this way, with people alternating between being givers and recipients.

For refreshments, have people draw slips from a hat that says what economic class they belong to. The slips are marked to reflect the proportions of rich, poor, and middle-class people found in the United States. The slip they draw determines whether they get crackers (for the poor people), donuts (for those in the middle), or really nice pastries (for the rich). See if people spontaneously approach others and ask or offer to share their treat. Discuss afterwards how people felt about this experience and how class impacts relationships within your faith community and across societal lines.[14]

TZEDAKAH COLLECTIVES AND
SOCIALLY RESPONSIBLE INVESTMENT

The historic pattern of giving in Jewish life in the form of tzedakah has translated in the past century to an increased emphasis on social action and poverty or crisis relief. This has led to the development of a variety of relief agencies such as the American Jewish World Service, the Jewish Committee on Disaster Relief, and the Joint

Distribution Committee of the United Jewish Communities, among others.

Many individuals, foundations, and faith communities seek to find new methods to express generosity financially as well as to give tzedakah that can have more long-term and deeper impact. In their book, *Tough Choices*, Rabbi David Saperstein and Alan Vorspan, both leaders in the area of social justice in the Jewish community, discuss the concept of "socially responsible investment" as an effective method of applying the values of tzedakah to a changing world.

Saperstein and Vorspan lay out two principles upon which social investment should be based. One is that individuals' or groups' financial investments should not implicate or group them in activities that would be considered immoral by the donors. Second, investments should be made in organizations and corporations whose activities are considered socially beneficial by the individual or group: cleaning the environment, increasing health care, strengthening education, providing affordable housing, promoting equal opportunities for all, and so forth. These proactive investment strategies allow investors to earn money while contributing to community development banks, loan funds, credit unions, as well as socially responsible mutual funds.[15]

In an article for *Sh'ma* magazine, Jeffery Dekro, president of the Shefa Fund, goes further to suggest that Jewish institutions must think of investments themselves as a form of tzedakah. Dekro notes that foundations that have invested their assets in socially responsible ways have found they are able to express their values more fully by supporting projects both inside and outside the Jewish community at a level far beyond their grant-making budgets. The Foundation for Jewish Community has long had a policy that at least 10 percent of all investment funds are used as low-income community development loans or bridge loans for nonprofits. The Shefa Fund's Tzedec initiative has mobilized more than $17 million in loans for housing and small business development, with a focus on minority and low-income neighborhoods. The Reform movement set a target of investing 1.8 percent of its assets for low-income community development.

Through shareholder activism, institutions can use their investment power to support greater corporate responsibility. As examples, Shefa's Jewish Shareholder Engagement Network, representing more than $1.3 billion in assets, has endorsed shareholder resolutions about prescription drug availability, response to HIV/AIDS in

Africa, equal opportunity, and the need for more transparent corporate governance.[16]

A tzedakah collective is a group of people who pool their funds
and decide together how to disburse them. Anybody can organize
one, though commonly they are formed within congregations or
existing *havurot* (fellowships) as independent groups. Giving through
a tzedakah collective can be more powerful and satisfying than giving as an individual. Combining gifts can be a way to create a large
impact on a small organization, or to respond in a powerful way to
a specific need. For example, Rabbi Eric Yoffie, leader of the Union
for Reform Judaism, encouraged members of Reform congregations
to form collectives to pool their tax rebate checks for tzedakah, resulting in greater impact in their donations, as well as increased aware-
ness of the meaning and power of tzedakah as a force for social
justice.

The tzedakah collective can also be about much more than pool-
ing funds. It can be the place where we talk about money, the most
taboo subject in our culture. The Jewish community, in particular,
needs safe places to candidly and honestly discuss money, a subject
weighted with significance for us as individuals and as a community.
We need to be able to reflect on both our success and on the role
money has played in anti-Semitic stereotypes that painfully persist to
this day. Tzedakah collectives are a place to address these issues. The
collective can also become the group that challenges the congregation itself to examine its financial practices concerning salaries, dues,
fund-raising, investing, and banking. When it comes time to disburse the tzedakah, we all have questions. How much for advocacy
and organizing to end poverty? For Jewish education? For Israel?
For the environment? The collective can be a place to think through
these and many other questions, learn about different organizations,
establish priorities, and even develop a long-term strategy for giving. Responding to such questions and issues fulfills the responsibility that our tradition places on us as stewards of wealth. Any person
can begin one by gathering friends; any congregation can start one.

Ultimately, of course, the purpose of the collective is to give
tzedakah, both to help those in need and to realize the powerful
spiritual component of giving in Jewish life. "Through the righ-
teousness of tzedakah I shall behold your face" (Ps. 17:15). "See
the immense power of tzedakah—for a person who gives a single
penny to the poor is deemed worthy to behold the face of the
Shechina [or "God's presence"]" (Tanhuma Leviticus 17a). Living

in the midst of a culture that encourages materialism and individual-
ism, conscious giving—encouraged by the group—can itself be an
act of liberation and of connection to the Divine.[17]

7

MONEY, VALUES, AND COMMUNITY

A Case Study

In the previous chapters we looked at our personal attitudes and experiences with money, examined Jewish tradition from various stages of the Jewish people's journey, and studied the progression from mission through planning, budgeting, dues, and fund-raising in communal life. At this point an important question to ask is how can a comprehensive Jewish values-based approach to money be applied in practice in a congregation or organization?

To answer this question I have chosen as a case study Dorshei Tzedek, Newton, Massachusetts, a fast-growing congregation of approximately 160 households. Rabbi Toba Spitzer, committee leader Wendy Gedanken, the lay leadership, and the membership's approach in this area have been inspirational. I also think it is valuable to look at a community that is modest in size, staffing, and infrastructure. From its inception, this community has taken to heart a Jewish values-based approach to decision making and put it into action in the area of money and congregational policy. This has allowed the congregation the time to develop an open, noncrisis, and driven culture around money.

I offer a description of Dorshei Tzedek's process, using details provided to me by Wendy Gedanken and materials from its Torah of Money committee. This is not meant to be a definitive approach, but rather one example of a participatory Jewish values-based approach to money in community. Different values will influence different approaches and outcomes. This is true whether these values are consciously or unconsciously reflected, made explicit or left implicit.

Dorshei Tzedek was founded in the early 1990s by a small group of people committed to growing a full-service congregation that included a religious school and a full-time rabbi. A great deal of dedication and effort, including a significant amount of volunteer labor that masked the true cost of services that members were receiving, led to the first stages of fulfilling this dream. While the congregation's programming and staffing increased significantly over the years, dues were kept low (approximately half those of other area synagogues). Additional fund-raising and some surpluses from earlier years made up the difference between expenses and income from membership dues. As the congregation grew and the staffing and programmatic needs increased, the challenge arose to raise the money to meet these new needs without making membership financially inaccessible to anyone, and to do so in a way that reflected who they were and wanted to be as a community.[1]

The leadership recognized that the challenge before them was how to raise sufficient funds in a manner consistent with their values. This would have been true whether their congregation was 100 or 1,000 households, volunteer dependent or fully staffed. In fact, creating a participatory process to articulate and own their values was itself a step important to them and their mission. While acknowledging that there is no perfect answer to this challenge, they delved into the process by learning from Jewish tradition and from the experience of other communities, and by engaging in serious discussion among the membership. In this way their community developed solutions that reflected the commitment and convictions of a majority of the congregation. They also knew that for any system to work, it needs the buy-in of all the membership, not only a select group in the process.

At the direction of the board, and by announcing the purpose and formation of a "Torah of Money" committee at services and in the congregational newsletter, a committee was formed with the mission to propose a new dues structure for the community that would reflect the values of the community. Some people were also invited to join the committee to ensure that the committee represented diverse viewpoints and demographics. Rabbi Toba Spitzer was responsible for Jewish text study.[2]

Once the committee was configured, they set to work defining what values (Jewish and larger societal) were key to informing decisions about raising and spending financial resources, and they analyzed how each value related to money. Building on the existing mission statement of the community, they studied texts from the Torah, Talmud, and contemporary sources (many of which are mentioned in chapter 1 of this book). One value in particular stood out for the committee members: *kedushah* or "holiness." As a religious community, members felt an ongoing desire to bring *kedushah* into daily life. Since money is a part of daily living, and therefore, depending on how it is used, can be a tool that brings the sacred into our lives, *kedushah* became the overarching objective.

They began by polling the congregation to learn exactly who they were economically. They devised a method to get specific income information on each family without knowing anyone's identity. Each household was assigned a number and that number was written on their questionnaire. As the questionnaires were returned in the mail, the secretary made a list of the numbers that came back. The questionnaires went off to whoever was collating the information. The list of numbers went to the chair of the Torah of Money committee, who had the list of members with the numbers. That way they could contact those who had not returned the questionnaire and ask them to return it. After the information was compiled, the list was destroyed. By being able to make a follow-up call, they were able to get an extraordinarily high return. They also made sure that they only asked about three questions, so the questionnaire was kept short. Since people do not generally talk about their income, they were unaware whether their assumptions about the wealth of the community were accurate. This data allowed them to create a table of suggested dues based on income that would bring in the money needed.

At the same time they asked their members, "What values would you like to see expressed in our dues structure?" and for any other comments. A variety of concerns surfaced in this process. People were afraid that if some people paid more dues than others, they would feel more "ownership," or those paying less would be second-class citizens. Some worried that dues would be too high and there was no way members in need would not feel some humiliation in asking for an abatement. Some worried that if they had a progressive structure, those at the high end would leave instead of paying high dues.

They held a series of small meetings in members' homes and over 40 percent of households participated. In planning for the meetings, they asked themselves what information they wished to share with the community and what information they hoped to learn from them. Questions included the following:

- How much of the congregational income should come from mandatory dues, versus voluntary contributions and other fund-raising?
- What kinds of considerations should go into determining the dues structure for a household income? Family makeup? Life circumstances?
- What are the core values that the community is committed to, which must be reflected in any system that is devised?

The committee's mandate was to synthesize the information and ideas gathered at the parlor meetings and make recommendations to the board for a new plan for dues and raising revenue.

To help people knowledgeably participate in the parlor meetings, the committee prepared a packet of materials, providing information that had been requested at a previous full membership meeting. This packet included the following:

- Congregational budget information
- Results of a survey of member income and a summary of previous discussions from membership meetings
- Information about average household income and synagogue dues levels in the greater Boston area
- Two articles written by committee members that gave the background on Jewish law and tradition regarding how Jewish communities have financially supported themselves
- Description of the committee's discussion of key values, and how these values might influence decisions on how to raise money

What follows are the two articles developed by members of their Torah of Money committee to help the committee and the membership in their values clarification process and discussions in the areas of dues and fund-raising.

THE HALAKHIC BASIS OF THE COMMUNITY FINANCING OF JEWISH LIFE

A Summary Meir Tamari's *With All Your Possessions:
Jewish Ethics and Economic Life*[3]

By Cliff Cohen

In virtually all societies, functions that lie beyond the domain or the capability of the individual are publicly financed. Jewish communities throughout history have assessed contributions for such functions from individual members, and Jewish tradition is rich with law and discussion about how to fairly distribute this burden. In this summary, as in the Tamari text on which it is based, the imposition of required contributions will be called "tax" or "Taxation"; in a modern sense, most of the concepts may be applied to the dues structure of a congregational community.

The Community's Responsibility and Rights

Any system that asserts the right of the community to assess property from the individual must be justified to its members. In Jewish thought, the core concept underlying such a right is society's responsibility for each of its members, down to the least fortunate—a responsibility that extends over and above the mitzvah of individual charity. Ultimately, the rabbis would extend this thinking so that the community (including its less fortunate members) has some rights to the property of all the individuals in the community.

The wellsprings of this communal power were to be found in *halakhik* text interpretations, which Tamari places in four general categories: the rights of neighbors (joint owners of adjacent property must cofinance common needs); the obligations of the citizen (each must contribute to the economic security of the whole); the rights of the king (kings in the Davidic line were empowered to take private property, with compensation, for the public good); and the law of the land (the government's law, if not illegal or discriminatory, was to be honored by the Jewish community). The result was a system of contributions for public functions—support of Torah study, building of cemeteries and synagogues, feeding the poor, supporting widows and orphans—which had the force of law, and was in fact enforced.

More importantly, concepts of basic equity among the inhabitants were promulgated. The level of taxation derived from the consent of the community. Tax evasion was the equivalent of theft from the other community members. Taxes were to be imposed by a formula that approximated fairness and equity. Widows, orphans, and the very poor were exempt from taxation. These concepts all had roots in Torah and its explication. They were interwoven with the three basic types of taxation, which historically were found in Jewish communities.

Types of Taxation

Over the centuries, taxes have been levied in three basic ways, and Jewish communities have employed all three: (1) the poll, per capita, or "flat" tax—each taxpayer pays the same amount or rate; (2) the excise tax or "user fee"—only the taxpayer who utilizes a service is taxed on the use of it; and (3) the "progressive" tax—a tax based on the income or wealth of the taxpayer. (It will easily be seen that a modern congregation may employ one, two, or three of these methods in raising the revenue necessary for functioning as well.)

Communal taxes based on income were unknown outside the Jewish world until the nineteenth century. In Jewish life, such taxes were known from antiquity. They were not pure income taxes as we know today, but were user taxes that were allocated based on the benefit derived—an allocation that in some cases was further tempered on the basis of wealth. An expense that protected the lives of all equally justified a per capita tax, but an expense that protected the property of the wealthy should result in a tax calculated according to wealth.

The sophistication of this system is illustrated by the rabbinic ruling on the cost of building a city wall. In medieval Europe, the wall was to protect property, not life, so a per capita tax was not justified. Therefore the rate of such tax should be based on wealth. But those who lived closer to the city's edge and the wall needed its protection more than those in the city center. So the tax was further apportioned to place the larger share of the total expense on those living close to the wall.

Of course with some functions, such as assistance to the poor, utility never entered the computation, and these taxes were based strictly on wealth. Why not per capita? Because, the rabbis said, those who possess wealth bear a greater moral responsibility to fund the needs of those who do not. Also, as to public expenses where everyone derives an equal benefit, such as the funding of a cantor's salary, the rich person must fund the poor person's pro rata share, simply because the poor person cannot fund his own. An additional wealth-based source of support for the poor was the tithe, a mandatory portion, usually one-tenth of one's income, which was paid every three years. It too featured a complex system of *halakhik* rules used to compute the exact amount.

The Tax Base and Exemptions

As noted above, Jewish values demanded that certain property be excluded from the tax base and certain persons exempt from taxation. Widows, orphans, and the poor were usually exempt. So, too, often were the disabled. Torah scholars were exempt. And the portion of a person's income set aside for making *aliyah* (literally "going up," but referring to moving to live in Israel) was exempted as well. In addition, newcomers were often given a year's grace.

Communal taxes were based on "equity," that is, the value of income-producing assets. The type of wealth taxed was carefully denoted so that property that did not produce income would not eventually be consumed by the tax. Therefore, personal belongings, one's residence, books, and monies set apart for charity, were not counted in the tax calculation.

In sum, the Jewish concept of taxation is democratic, compassionate, nonconfiscatory, and in many instances progressive. One of the primary purposes of such taxation is publicly funding the transmission, study, and preservation of Jewish values, ritual, and community. Taxes, when imposed, are mandatory because the community has the right to make them so. A failure to fulfill one's mandated responsibility, therefore, is theft from the community. Fundamental to traditional Jewish economics is an understanding that, ultimately, all of our wealth has its origins with God, and our enjoyment of that wealth is conditional upon how we use it. Each Jewish community is challenged, therefore, to use its collective resources well, and to be fair and thoughtful in how it decides to raise the monies needed for its well-being.

BUILDING A WALL AND THE WINTER MEMBER'S MEETING

By Clifford Goldsmith

Dorshei Tzedek became involved in a year-long program of discussion and study around our material life as a community, a process which culminated with a proposal from the board and a vote by the membership for a new, values-based dues structure.

The first meeting began with Rabbi Toba Spitzer leading a discussion about the way that money flows to and from each of us in our daily living. Toba asked participants to partner up and discuss Rabbi Ishmael's statement "One who wishes to acquire wisdom should study the ways of society [that is, the way that money works] for there is no greater area of Torah study than this. It is like an ever-flowing stream" (Babylonian Talmud, *Bava Batra* 175b). Participants then discussed together the ways in which the "flow" of money into and out of a community might tell us interesting things about that community, including its values and priorities, where power lies, and the relationships among the members and between the community and the world outside.

Participants were provided with an interesting perspective on the financial history of Dorshei Tzedek and the rapid growth that the community has experienced in recent years. Cliff Cohen explained how the project began and how a group of nine congregants have worked through issues before expanding the study to the whole community. Finally, members were asked to break up into small groups and to discuss a few questions. One of these questions was "what would you like someone from outside our congregation to learn about us from the way we raise and spend our money?"

In attempting to answer that question, Cliff invited participants to look at another community and understand the values that they applied to raising funds. Using the ancient rabbinic approach of *midrash* (teaching through parable and sermon) connected to Jewish tradition, Cliff invited participants to imagine a Jewish community living nearly 2,000 years ago that he developed as a parable, as they wrestled with their own issues of money and Jewish values. The following is that "modern midrash":[4]

> It is the year 120 CE. For more than a hundred years now, a small community of Jews living in Sek, Palestine, has been burdened by excessive Roman taxation and outraged by acts of Roman brutality. The Sek community had come very close to losing their Jewish

identity, but in recent years the Roman emperor's policies had become milder and the community's rabbi had rallied the people to reconstruct their religious and social lives.

The leaders of Sek decided that they needed a wall around their little village to protect them from the bands of roving Romans that were still attacking Jewish settlements. The question that soon arose was exactly how would the community fund the building of this wall? The leaders resorted to a study of money and Jewish values for answers.

Sek, a community of almost 200 families, had the typical distribution of wealth. There was a handful of very wealthy and a handful of very poor, with the majority of people being distributed between the two extremes. Most Sek families had been part of the community for several years, but a few had recently moved from their tormented villages to this supportive community. Most townspeople owned a home, but some rented rooms from other members of the community. Some participated in community activity and others chose to keep more to themselves.

After extensive study and discussion, the leaders decided that everyone in the community would benefit from the protection of the wall. They therefore compelled every member of the Sek community, rich or poor, to contribute to the building of the surrounding wall, folding doors and a cross bar. Townspeople who had lived in the community for less than one year were not required to participate in the levy unless they purchased or built a house during that time. The only other exemption was the rabbi since it was believed that he did not need the protection of the wall (but that is another whole story!).

The issue then turned to exactly how much each person would pay. Being acutely aware of the injustice of the flat, poll tax system of the Romans, the Sek leaders decided that each should be levied according to their means. But this was not the only factor that accounted for the exact levy each villager paid. From other reports we understand that the levy was further modified based on the resident's proximity to the wall. The people of Sek contributed and thus the wall was built.

Let us assume that this is all we know about how the leaders of Sek levied their townspeople to build a protective wall for their village. What can we learn about their values from the way that they decided to raise the money for their town wall?

We learn that Sek chose a mechanism of raising funds whereby those who benefit should share equally in the funding. In the case of the protective wall, all members derived benefit and therefore all were required to contribute.

However, *we also learn* that determining the degree of benefit is not so simple. Benefit does not accrue to all people equally. The wall was built around the town to protect the inhabitants from thieves, and the cost of the wall was determined by what is protected—people's property. Rather than an equal tax per capita, the tax was determined proportional to wealth. Furthermore, those living at the perimeter derived greater benefit than those at the center since their property was more vulnerable, and so they were required to contribute more.

We learn that the people of Sek were thoughtful and just. They had recently experienced the injustice of the Roman poll tax, which required everyone to pay the same amount, placing a disproportional burden on the poor. Sek leaders opted to levy each according to their means. *We also learn* from the decisions of Sek that they respected the poor, by requiring that they pay at least a small amount for public services from which they derive benefit. As Rabbah taught, "I collect from them in order to give them a better standing" (Babylonian Talmud, *Bava Batra* 8a).

We learn further that the community of Sek understood the process of integration with the community and thus they exempted newcomers from the levy. People who had yet not demonstrated a commitment to live in the village by either length of stay or a binding purchase were not required to contribute to the wall.

We learn that communal expenditure is a complex process. Sek is clearly a tightly-knit community, and part of the consideration in paying the levy comes from a sense of obligation for the community as a whole rather than each person's benefit as an individual.

We can see a community in two ways. One is that the community is the sum of its members. Within this view a community purchase is simply a purchase by the individuals involved in the community. If one had no need to purchase the item and could be excluded from its benefit or, truly had no benefit, then an argument could be made for this individual not to be considered one of the purchasers and therefore not to have to pay.

Yet, the community is an entity unto itself, where the whole is greater than the sum of its parts. The community has obligations and purchases that the community must undertake as a responsible

Jewish community. Members of the community have a responsibility to act in order for the community to meet its goal. This is like the many *mitzvot* that fall on the *kahal* (community or defined group) whereby the individual is commanded to do what is necessary to ensure that the community meets its obligations.

What are our community's walls, or our communal expenses? What protects us? Is it our Hebrew school that gives our children a wonderful education, so that our Jewish traditions survive into the next generation, and continue to deepen and evolve? Is it our religious services, led by our rabbi and lay leaders that offer us spiritual renewal and shelter from the vicissitudes of daily life? Is it our adult and family education that helps us grow and flourish? Is it our nurturing community that gives us strength?

How will we raise funds for our wall? I am sure of one answer: with thought and study, and with a continued commitment to our values as a community.

Along with the readings and research that members were given ahead of time, the committee presented three different models at the parlor meetings: a modified flat structure; an income-based structure; and a hybrid that we called half-shekel or *nadiv lev* (offering of the heart) model.[5]

Modified flat creates categories based on factors such as marital status, children, age, new members, and so on. A sliding scale looks at income by setting either a fixed percentage of income, or a graduating scale, often between 1 to 3 percent, that increases by income category. The half-shekel/*nadiv lev* model takes its name from two passages in Exodus. The half-shekel was a census tax. Every adult male was expected to pay exactly one half-shekel, no matter the individual's wealth. All were equal. *Nadiv lev* refers to the requirement that the Israelites give offerings to build the *mishkan* (sanctuary) based on their individual heart's desire. As presented in the parlor meetings, this model had three components: a small amount that was the same per member, another amount that was based on income, and a third amount (what we were calling *nadiv lev*) that the committee and board hoped members would be moved to contribute.

At the end of the parlor meetings, participants were asked to fill out a short questionnaire asking them if they preferred a particular plan, whether they found the meeting helpful, and what else they wanted to tell us.

The parlor meetings were very useful. They gave a forum for the general membership to share their thoughts; they helped committee members clarify their thinking.

After the parlor meetings, and conversations with the executive committee and the board, a revised *nadiv lev* (giving heart or generous spirit) model was developed that was composed of a contemporary version of the half-shekel per adult member, the remainder of dues based on a sliding scale, and an understanding that without additional contributions, the congregation could not meet its obligations.[6] One thing that changed was their understanding of *nadiv lev*. An understanding arose that whether it is a contribution or dues, the hope is that the money is given in the spirit of *nadiv lev*.

As well, the committee periodically shared their progress and emerging insights with the congregation through articles in their newsletter. In addition, Rabbi Spitzer used forums such as a members meeting to engage in Torah study with the larger community. The following is the values list that the community developed and the framework for dues they established as a result of their process.

GOALS

Dorshei Tzedek is a caring and inclusive Jewish community. We are committed to seriously and creatively engaging with Jewish texts and tradition and to making Judaism meaningful in our lives and in the lives of our members. Our goal is to build a dynamic, financially stable congregation that reflects the overriding Jewish values of *kedushah* or "holiness." We seek to infuse our financial structure with the values of Jewish tradition and Reconstructionist Judaism, and to affirm the spiritual as well as practical aspects of our dealings with money.

VALUES

To achieve these goals, we have identified key values that guide our decision making around financial issues. These include:

B'TZELEM ELOHIM (HUMAN DIGNITY)

One of the most fundamental values taught in the Torah and expanded upon in the rabbinic tradition is that every person is created in God's image (see Gen. 1:27). No matter what a person's circumstances, one must never be denied his or her dignity.

KEHILLAH (COMMUNITY)

Jewish tradition stresses individual obligation to the community and communal responsibility for its individual members. Traditionally, every Jew is responsible for helping maintain the Jewish community in which she or he lives, learns, and worships.

NADIV LEV (GENEROSITY)

When the ancient Israelites came together to build the *mishkan* (tabernacle) in the desert, they were asked to bring offerings of *nadiv lev*, literally, a "willing heart and mind." The Torah emphasizes that the *mishkan* was built through the generous outpouring of the Israelites hearts and hands (see Exod. 35:20-29). As a community, we wish to foster a culture of *nadiv lev* in which giving is a joyful responsibility.

ACCESSIBILITY AND DIVERSITY

We strive to be an inclusive, welcoming, and diverse community. To that end, we affirm the importance of being financially accessible to all who wish to join. We also acknowledge the diversity of class background and income level within the larger Jewish community, and welcome that diversity in our congregation.

DEMOCRACY

We affirm the equal value of every member to the community and the importance of participation by all, regardless of financial means.

TZEDEK (JUSTICE AND FAIRNESS)

Recognizing that wealth is distributed unequally in our society, it is important that we take into account the differing financial resources of our members and structure the dues system accordingly. We also see our own dealings with money as reflecting a larger commitment to create a more just and fair world.

FROM THE TRADITION

Judaism seeks to infuse a sense of awe and sacred obligation into all aspects of our lives—including our material lives. Jewish tradition finds nothing inherently positive or negative about money; what is important is how we deal with it and use it.

Over the past two thousand years, Jewish communities have continued to wrestle with the issue of how to pay for communal necessities, from rabbis' and cantors' salaries, to physical infrastructure, to charity funds. In studying texts from many periods of our history, we learned that Jewish communities have survived by creating mutual agreements to tax themselves, based on the understanding that the individual and the community are responsible for each other.

While the wealthier members of the community were expected to take on a larger portion of the financial burden, even the poorest members of the community were given the opportunity to contribute something to maintain their dignity and to affirm the values of giving.

OUR DUES STRUCTURE

Congregation Dorshei Tzedek is committed to raising the funds we need to support our programs in a way that is consonant with our values as a community. The following principles shape our revenue-raising structure:

- The equal value of each member to the community, and the importance of individual responsibility to the community
- A commitment to fairness, by taking into account the differing financial resources of our members
- Fostering a culture of generous giving

Another value that we affirm in this system is trust of one another. The information on the income form is confidential (amounts will only be seen by the administrator and the treasurer), and we trust each member to honestly self-assess on the sliding scale. We realize that life circumstances might affect ability to pay at any given time, and that this might affect your self-assessment. No one will be denied membership because of financial hardship (please call the rabbi or the treasurer if you need to make special arrangements). At the same time, we expect that those who have greater ability to contribute at any given time will do so.

Each of the above principles is reflected in one component of the revenue structure. Each adult member is assessed a *hatzi shekel* of $100, symbolizing each individual's commitment to this community and the equal "buy-in" of each member.

Each household is assessed a portion of its income for the remainder of the dues obligation, along a progressive sliding scale according to gross household income, with each member paying approximately 1 to 1.3 percent of his or her income in dues.

Finally, all members are asked to consider giving a gift of *nadiv lev*, a generosity offering that reflects your willingness and ability to give. Because of the cap on the sliding scale, our members in the highest income category pay the lowest percentage of their income in dues. We would ask those members to especially consider making a contribution above and beyond dues.

New Members

The Talmud teaches that a new person in a community is given time to settle in, and is not immediately responsible for all the taxes of that community (Babylonian Talmud, *Bava Batra* 8a). In accordance with that teaching, we ask people joining our congregation to pay approximately half of the regular dues in the first year of membership.

Although the congregation had no conflicts about the values they articulated in the beginning of their process, there was not consensus either in the committee or in the community about how to translate those values into a workable and dependable revenue-raising plan. Feelings were strong, and people spoke passionately. In the end, there was recognition that what they were doing was an experiment and was not written in stone.

The single most contentious issue involved the income cap at the top range ($2,500). On the one side were those who felt that a cap was necessary, in order not to scare away potential new members with greater financial resources. Those opposed to a cap felt that it placed an unfair burden on those in the middle to mid-upper incomes. They were concerned that these households would be stretching just to pay the dues, and would have nothing left over for contributions. Ultimately the message to those who are at the top income level is a reminder that they are paying a lower percentage of their income than others and should take that into consideration when they decide what their *nadiv lev* contribution will be.

Dorshei Tzedek did not lose members because of the change in dues structure. Nor did the changes in its dues structure deter people from joining since it continues to grow. They worked hard at including the whole community in the education and discussion. It was clear early on in their process that they would never reach 100 percent unanimity in what the best design would be. This meant that the process became very important. The leadership did not want to see members leave because they felt they weren't heard. The Torah of Money committee members were careful to always speak and listen respectfully and they set a tone for discussion that spread to the greater community. Another major impact for the congregation has been to develop a model of a Jewish values-based way for them to make major decisions regardless of the issue at hand.

The congregational leadership viewed this study as an opportunity for the community to grow, and to grow together. They recognized that they had to keep this in mind and make sure that all discussions were conducted in a respectful manner so that everyone felt safe to express their opinions. What everyone gained in this process is now being applied to the areas of capital campaigns and fundraising.

Lastly, they recently reconvened their "Torah of Money" committee to look at the issues surrounding *nadiv lev.* They wrestled quite a bit with the term. What does it mean to be obligated to make a donation? One answer to this question involves going back to the Hebrew Bible, where the heart is not viewed as the seat of feelings, but rather of wisdom. What if your heart is not moved to give? Offerings of the heart are not determined by emotional inclination alone, but are motivated by a well-thought-out conscious approach to giving. A person looks at what the need is and figures out what they think is the right amount to give based on some combination of need and ability. "Feeling good" comes from knowing you have acted from a place of *kedushah* (holiness) and that your actions are contributing to the strengthening of these values throughout the congregational system.

As I mentioned in the beginning of this chapter, the Dorshei Tzedek approach is only one of many that communities across North America have been developing. The variety of approaches are informed by the legacy of the Jewish people across centuries, and influenced by the participatory democratic culture we all live in today. The process Dorshei Tzedek undertook, and continues to follow, was both possible and successful because there was already a clear sense of the mission of the congregation and the role values play in creating and sustaining sacred community.

In your congregation, fellowship, or organization, a clarification of the mission and vision of the group and a general discussion and study of core values may be a necessary first step before tackling an issue such as dues or fund-raising. You may look to your own bylaws and existing policies around membership or ritual life for an understanding of how you are already living out your religious and cultural self-definition.

Ultimately a Jewish values-based process such as the one outlined in this chapter cannot be a one-time exploration. The process also includes exploring congregational policies, sense of "obligation" and clarification of membership, ideals, focus, and so on. Each project, as well as each generation, is the canvas upon which the articles of faith are being drawn in the legacy of spiritual peoplehood. What processes and what outcomes will determine your congregation or organization's legacy?

Epilogue

TOWARDS A BEGINNING

A Prayer

We have a tradition that one is not poor
unless they lack knowledge.
—Babylonian Talmud, *Nedarim* 41a

Money flows through your life and touches every aspect.
Although you have only so much control of how it flows into
your life, how money flows out from your life, just like how you
spend your time, reflects your values and what you hold precious.
We shouldn't be embarrassed that it takes money to run a
synagogue—we should be happy to see that our financial support
has created an extraordinary community that we value dearly.
—Jeff Deitch from a newsletter of
Congregation Beth Israel, Media, Pennsylvania

Midrash Rabbah, the classic source of ancient rabbinic homilies and
teachings, unfolds this simple metaphor about the flow of giving
and receiving, into a more complete and beautiful teaching:

There are two seas in the land of Israel.
One is fresh, and fish are in it.
Splashes of green adorn its bands.
Trees spread their branches over it,
And stretch their thirsty roots
To sip of its healing waters.

113

Along its shores, children play.
The River Jordan makes this sea sparkle
With water from the hills.
It laughs in the sunshine.
People build their homes near to it,
And birds their nests;
And every kind of life is happier
Because it is there.

The River Jordan also flows south into another sea.
Here there is no splash
Of fish, no fluttering leaf,
No song of birds, no children's laughter.
Travelers choose another route
Unless on urgent business.
The air hangs heavily above its waters,
And neither person nor beast nor fowl will drink.

What makes this mighty difference in these seas?
Not the River Jordan.
It empties the same good water into both.
Not the soil in which they lie.
Not the country round about.

This is the difference.
The Sea of Galilee receives
But does not keep the Jordan.
For every drop that flows into it,
Another drop flows out.
The giving and receiving
Go on in equal measure.
The other sea however, is shrewd,
Hoarding its income jealously.
It will not be tempted
Into any generous impulse.
Every drop it gets, it keeps.
It lets nothing flow out.
The Sea of Galilee gives and lives.
The other sea gives nothing.
It is called
The Dead Sea.[1]

Blessed are you, Source of Abundance,
for providing us with the financial
and spiritual ability to give.
You reveal to us in our actions
that all humanity participates
in the flow of resources that come
and go through the world.
May we use our resources well,
and may this exchange be fair and equal.
Blessed are you, Provider,
who is the enriching Power of Life itself.[2]

Appendix

SAMPLE LESSON

Introducing Your Membership to Jewish Values, Money, and Your Community

By Rabbi Shawn Zevit and Shira Stutman

Portions of this lesson are from Jewish Values, Money and Your Community, *a 12-week curriculum developed for the Jewish Reconstructionist Federation, 2003.*

The following is offered as an example of how to take some of the approaches of this book into action in your congregation. This is a foundational exercise and can be facilitated by clergy, educators, or skilled lay leaders.

GOALS

- Introduce group to the issues
- Introduce participants to each other
- Explore personal attitudes towards money and wealth
- Learn more about your community

WELCOME

Time needed: 15 minutes

- Introductions, discussion on creating a safe space and a community of learners

- Go-round: What provides wealth or abundance for you?
- Discussion: How much of what provides wealth/abundance has to do with money? What can we learn from these observations?

EXPLORING PERSONAL ATTITUDES

Rabbi Shawn Zevit,
adapted from material developed by the Alban Institute

Time needed: 45 minutes

Questions that can be circulated on a separate sheet for study in small groups or for private use, either sent ahead of the session or distributed at the time.

Because these questions are personal in nature, reading them to each other in study pairs *(hevrutah)* or small groups, then reporting back to the larger group which questions drew the most interest and why, is one way to approach this exercise. Additional time can also be given for participants to write responses to the questions, then in small groups or one large group, summarize what responding brought up for them and some general trends they noticed or learning they took away from the exercise. For any faith community or organization, simply substitute your religious group where appropriate.

- If I were to share one thing about money and me with someone else, what would it be?
- What dreams do I have that I think money will help make possible?
- How is my sense of safety and security tied up with money?
- Would I feel less valued if I had less money, or more valued if I had more money? Why?
- How was money discussed in my childhood home?
- With whom am I most (and least) comfortable speaking about money? Why?
- When in my life have I been least concerned about money? Why then?
- When in my life have I been most concerned about money? Why then?
- Who is the most generous person I know? How has that person extended his or her generosity?

- How does your experience or understanding of God and Judaism connect to your spending and income generation?
- When you were growing up, did you feel that you had enough, less than enough, or more than enough money in your home? How was this experienced or communicated to you?
- What hesitations do you feel about applying Jewish principles to your most significant financial activities? Which of your values would you simply not compromise in the name of profit?
- What measures might you, your social networks, your business, your Jewish community, or your society undertake to help you commit to a "covenanted" economic life?

After discussing the questions above, proceed in the large group with the following:

- Before talking about decision making, we encourage exploration of our personal attitudes towards money.
- Facilitator asks the group: In a word or two, what were some of the messages about money you received growing up? (Facilitator or other participant writes words on large paper. Give people a moment to think, and after each few responses invite more until you sense the group is done or you decide to move on.)
- What are the messages about money that you receive from popular culture and mass media today? (Facilitator or other participant writes words on a new page of paper.)
- What are the messages you've received about Jews, Judaism, and money? (Facilitator or other participant writes words on a new page of paper.)
- Put the pieces together, give the group a minute to look them over, and discuss. What are the contradictions or tensions? What are the overlaps? Which messages do you appreciate?

PRESENTATION

Time needed: 15 minutes

The History of Our Congregation (with an emphasis on financial and programmatic aspects)

- Read and discuss synagogue mission statement or statement of principles and some of your community's history around money (such as fund-raising, tzedakah, and so forth).
- Having explored your personal attitudes and begun to examine your congregation's history and values around money and religious life, we conclude with a final exercise that helps us examine how our personal interaction with money intersects with our values and actions as a faith community.
- The exercise below is another way of examining your personal relationship with money and how that enhances or complicates your relationship to money in your faith community. Read the Talmudic text, and then on a piece of paper complete the exercise below, concluding in a group by answering the questions afterwards.

> Rabbi Ishmael said: One who wishes to acquire wisdom should study the ways of society, for there is no greater area of Torah study than this. It is like an ever-flowing stream. (Babylonian Talmud, *Bava Batra* 175b)

- Fill out the diagram, indicating the sources from which money flows to you, and the destinations to which your money goes (for example, in-flow from a job, inheritance, investments, government payments; out-flow to merchants, taxes, schools, tzedakah, and so forth). Try to be as complete as possible.

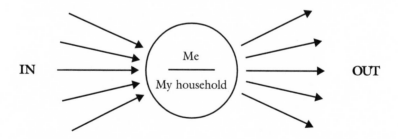

- In your *hevruta* (study partnership) or small group, discuss the following:

  — Following Rabbi Ishmael's teaching, what wisdom could you acquire by studying the flow of money in your life? What would you learn?

— Why does Rabbi Ishmael consider this a "great area of Torah study"? In what ways can understanding the workings of money be considered Torah (that is, sacred text)?
— What is similar or different in how money flows in your household compared to your congregation or organization?

CLOSING

Time needed: 10 minutes

• What were your insights this session about your attitudes toward money and community? Jewish values and approaches to money in community? What questions did it raise for future discussions?

For the full curriculum, contact the Jewish Reconstructionist Federation toll-free at (877) 573-7827. You can also visit the Federation's Web site at www.jrf.org for more information.

NOTES

PREFACE

1. See Deuteronomy 14:22, later extended in both Rabbinic Judaism and Christian thought.

2. See Genesis 1:26-27. This idea of humanity (male and female) being created in the Divine image gives rise to the later Kabbalistic and Hadisic idea that each human being, each part of creation itself, contains a spark of God within.

3. The word *parnaseem* is the plural of *parnas,* meaning a supporter, administrator, or leader of a community. The word is also related to *parnasah,* which means "livelihood," "upkeep," "provision," and "support." The sustaining of personal and communal resources is directly linked in the Hebrew to the concept of leadership.

4. I am consciously not using the translation of *tzedakah* as "charity" in this book, which I believe undermines the intent of tzedakah in Jewish thought and practice. Tzedakah is not money given to those who have less by those who have more. It implies a foundation of social and economic justice that is everyone's concern regardless of his or her material resources or financial means. See chapter 6 in this book for more on the topic of tzedakah.

5. *Halakhah* is usually translated as "Jewish law," including Jewish values, traditions, and customs—sacred ways in the broader sense.

6. Rabbi Mordecai Kaplan, in both *Judaism as a Civilization* (New York: Jewish Publication Society, 1994) and *The Future of the American Jew* (New York: MacMillan, 1948), outlined his thinking towards creating a comprehensive program for the ongoing reconstruction of creative Jewish life. His ideas about the organic nature of community and the evolving nature of Judaism as both a religion and a culture have been of great influence to contemporary Jewish life in North America as well as my views of how Jewish community and tradition function.

7. Maimonides, Mishneh Torah, Hilchot De'ot, Chapter 5, Halachah 13.

CHAPTER 1

1. Reviewing Meir Tamari's book *With All Your Possessions: Jewish Ethics and Economic Life,* the chapter on money in Rabbi Arthur Waskow's *Down-to-Earth Judaism,* and Larry Bush and Jeffery Dekro's coedited book, *Jews, Money and Social Responsibility,* can also be immensely helpful. A 12-week curriculum to educate congregational leadership that Shira Stuttman and I developed for the Jewish Reconstructionist Federation takes you through this educational process in a wide range of congregational financial issues. These books are all listed in further resources at the end of this volume. There are also good resources available through the Reform (Union for Reform Judaism) and Conservative (United Synagogues of Conservative Judaism) movements, the Orthodox Caucus's Tzedakah and Tzedek report, the Jewish Funder's Network, ZIV Foundation, the United Jewish Communities, the Center for Leadership and Learning (CLAL), as well as other Jewish organizations (see resource section for more details).

2. The word *mishkan* (dwelling place) comes from the three-letter Hebrew root word *sh-ch-n.* Derivatives of this word include *shochen* (to dwell), *shichunah* (neighborhood), and *shechinah* (the immanent, in-dwelling presence of God). There is a deep connection here between the intimate experience of God's presence in our lives, the places we live together in community, and the holy spaces we build to focus and raise consciousness around the ultimate source of our lives. This is a Jewish value that applied to the Divine center of the Israelites during their years of wandering, the temple of ancient Jerusalem, and the contemporary temple, synagogue, or *havurah.*

3. Pirke Avot, *Ethics of the Sages,* 1:1.

4. Leonard Kravitz and Kerry Olitzky, *Pikre Avot: A Modern Commentary on Jewish Ethics* (New York: UAHC Press, 1998), 94.

5. Interpretive translation of Mishna Berachot 9:5, Shawn Zevit.

6. See Exodus 22:20-21; 23:4-9; Leviticus 19:9-10, 33-34; and Deuteronomy 16:20 for additional references to justice and sharing resources.

7. David Saperstein and Albert Vorspan, *Tough Choices* (New York: URJ Press, 1992), 181.

8. Ibid., 181–82. The societies referred to are called "agencies" today.

9. Bachya Ibn Pakuda, *Duties of the Heart,* trans. Yaakov Feldman (Northvale, N.J.: Jason Aronson Inc., 1996), 177–78.

10. Babylonian Talmud, Avodah Zarah 17b. Rabbi Chaninah administered a charity fund. When an error occurred, he replaced the money out of his own pocket.

11. Babylonian Talmud, Yevamot 109a.

12. Rabbi Yehudah HeChasid, *Sefer Chasidim,* trans. Avraham Finkel (Northvale, N.J.: Jason Aronson Inc., 1997), 116, 193 (330-1).

13. Rabbi Nilton Bonder, *The Kabbalah of Money: Insights on Livelihood, Business, and All Forms of Economic Behavior* (Boston and London: Shambhala, 1996), 37.

14. Ibid., 14, 15.

15. Moshe Chayim Luzzato, Mesilat Yesharim, Chapter 21.

16. Keter Shem Tov, 91.

17. Schmuel of Sochochow, *Shem mi shmuel, parshat shelach*, as quoted in Meir Tamari's *The Challenge of Wealth* (Northvale, N.J.: Jason Aronson Inc., 1995), 15.

18. Rabbi A. I. HaKohen Kook, *Shabbat Ha'aretz*, as quoted in Meir Tamari's *The Challenge of Wealth*, 23–24.

19. Ninth blessing of the weekday *Amidah*; translation from *Kol Haneshamah, Limnot Hol* Daily Prayerbook (Wyncote, Pa.: The Reconstructionist Press, 1996), 228.

20. Ibid., 234.

21. Adaptation of translation from "Birkat Hamazon," the Jewish prayer of thanksgiving after meals, *Art Scroll Siddur* (Brooklyn, N.Y.: Mesorah Publications, 1988), 191.

22. Translation from *Kol Haneshamah, Shabbat Verasim* (Wyncote, Pa.: The Reconstructionist Press, 1996), 416.

23. Rabbi Benjamin Arnold, *The Sinai Dialogue*, newsletter of Temple Sinai, Amherst, N.Y. (December 2000).

24. Rabbi Abraham Joshua Heschel, *The Sabbath* (New York: Noonday Press, 1991).

25. See n. 19.

CHAPTER 2

1. Rabbi Kalonymus Kalman Shapira, *Conscious Community*, trans. Andrea Cohen-Kiener (Northvale, N.J.: Jason Aaronson Inc., 1996), 3–5.

2. Martin Buber, *I and Thou* (New York: Charles Scribner and Sons, 1970), 94.

CHAPTER 3

1. See examples of a mission statement process in chapter 2 and the case study in chapter 7.

2. Mordecai Kaplan, *The Future of the American Jew*, as quoted in the *Rabbi-Congregational Report: A Vision for the 21st century*, Rabbi Richard Hirsh, ed. (report of the role of the rabbi commission of the Reconstructionist Movement, Elkins Park, Pa.: Reconstructionist Press, Fall 2000), 148.

3. Hirsh, ed., *The Rabbinic-Congregation Relationship*.

CHAPTER 4

1. See Exodus 30 on the half-shekel; Exodus 35 on freewill offerings; and Leviticus 19 and Deuteronomy 14, 24, and 26 on tithing.

2. The Mishnah, "Pirket Avot," *Ethics of the Sages,* 3:17.

3. Meir Tamari, *With All Your Possessions: Jewish Ethics and Economic Life* (Northvale, N.J.: Jason Aaronson Inc., 1998).

4. Lawrence Bush and Jeffrey Dekro are co-authors of *Jews, Money and Social Responsibility.*

5. See Bob Leventhal and Rabbi Shawn Zevit, "Money and Spiritual Life," in *Congregations* (November/December 2001), 9.

6. Excerpted from Rabbi Shawn Zevit, "Synagogue Dues with Less Blues," in *Reconstructionism Today* 10, no. 3 (Spring 2003).

7. From www.kolhalev.net, the Web site of the Kol HaLev, Cleveland, 2000, courtesy of Arnie Berger.

CHAPTER 5

1. See Joyce Norden, "Tzedakah and Community," *The Reconstructionist* 4 (Winter 1997).

2. The Shefa Fund is a Jewish values-based funding and fund collection organization based in Philadelphia.

3. Jewish Reconstructionist Congregation capital campaign letter, April 7, 2003, Evanston, Ill.

4. Rabbi Yehudah HeChasid, *Sefer Chasidim,* trans. Avraham Finkel, (189/324) (Northvale, N.J.: Jason Aronson Inc., 1997), 118.

5. Dan Hotchkiss, *Ministry and Money* (Bethesda, Md.: Alban Institute, 2002), 31.

6. Shulchan Aruch, Orach Chayim 151:1 quoting "Happy are they who sit in Your house." (Ps. 84:5).

7. Rabbi Daniel Feldman, "Be Pure Before GOD and Israel," Tzedakah, Inc., and the Orthodox Caucus, 2002; Jewish sources based on Matteh Efraim 607:7, Mishpetei Hatorah III, 20:6, Babylonian Talmud, Bava Batra 8b, Shluchan Aruch Yoreh Deah 248:1, 7, Aruch Hashulchan 248:15.

8. Ibid.; Jewish sources based on Babylonian Talmud *Nedarim* 28a, *Gittin* 10b, *Bava Kama* 113a, *Bava Batra* 54b.

9. Rabbi Arthur Waskow, *Down to Earth Judaism: Food, Money, Sex, and the Rest of Life.* (New York: William Morrow and Co., 1995), 222.

CHAPTER 6

1. Randall M. Falk and Walter J. Harrelson, *Jews and Christians in Pursuit of Social Justice* (Nashville: Abingdon Press, 1996), 138.

2. Charles R. Strain, *Prophetic Visions and Economic Realities* (Grand Rapids: William Eerdman's Publishing Co., 1989), 90.

3. Rabbi Toba Spitzer, *Beyond Charity: Rabbinic Approaches to Economic Justice* (unpublished manuscript, 2000).

4. Babylonian Talmud, Yevamot, 47a.

5. Strain, *Prophetic Visions and Economic Realities*, 81.

6. "Do not let him come down until he falls completely, for then it will be difficult to raise him. Instead, uphold him at the time he begins to fall," as quoted in A. Ben Isaiah and B. Sharfman, *The Pentateuch and Rashi's Commentary: Leviticus* (New York: SS & R Publishing, 1949), 265.

7. Rabbi Yehudah HeChasid, *Sefer Chasidim,* trans. Avraham Finkel (Northvale, N.J.: Jason Aronson Inc., 1997), 114–15. A wordplay in Hebrew contrasting the word for justice *(tzedakah)* and crying out *(tze'akah)*; this phrasing is also found in Isaiah 5:7: "He hoped for justice, but behold outcry!" The last line is quoting the Babylonian Talmud, *Bava Metzia* 71a: "If the choice lies between donating to your poor relatives or the general poor of the town—your relatives come first."

8. Ibid., 198 (1004) (189/324), 118–19.

9. The *Baal Shem Tov* (Master of the Good name), Keter Shem Tov, p. 109, as quoted in Yitzhak Buxbaum, *Jewish Spiritual Practices* (Northvale, N.J.: Jason Aronson Inc., 1990), 458–59. The Baal Shem Tov or *Besht* is the founder of Chasidism in seventeenth-century Eastern Europe.

10. Strain, *Prophetic Visions and Economic Realities,* 85.

11. Ibid., 87.

12. Maimonides, Mishneh Torah, Gifts to the Poor 10:7-14.

13. Bob Barkin, *The Power of Tzedakah* (unpublished manuscript, Adat Shalom, Bethesda, Md., March 2003).

14. I thank Rabbis Josh Lesser, Shana Margolin, Bob Tabak, and David Steinberg for some of these ideas. Danny Siegel, a leader in tzedakah programming and distribution, has many more ideas and group activities, as well as a special bar/bat mitzvah section at www.ziv.org.

15. David Saperstein and Albert Vorspan, *Tough Choices* (New York: URJ Press, 1992), 187–88.

16. Jeffery Dekro, "Investing Assets as Tzedakah," in *Sh'ma: A Journal of Jewish Responsibility* (February 2005). www.shma.org.

17. Mordechai Liebling, "Tzedakah Collectives," *Sh'ma: A Journal of Jewish Responsibility* (October 2001). Rabbi Mordechai Liebling is Torah of Money Director at The Shefa Fund, and former executive director of the Jewish Reconstructionist Federation. Some ideas for his article are based on Betsy Tessler and Jeffrey Dekro, *Building Community, Creating Justice: A Guide for Organizing Tzedakah Collectives* (Philadelphia: The Shefa Fund, 1994).

CHAPTER 7

1. This process began in 1999, resulting in a new plan for dues and fund-raising in 2000 to 2001, as well as an ongoing examination of how to

approach fund-raising in general and a capital campaign over the next few years.

2. This chapter incorporates material and interviews provided by Wendy Gedanken, chair of the "Torah of Money" committee and Rabbi Toba Spitzer of Dorshei Tzedek, a member community of the Jewish Reconstructionist Federation in Newton, Massachusetts.

3. Cliff Cohen was a member of the Dorshei Tzedek "Torah of Money" committee and summarized Meir Tamari's book for the committee and congregational study. Meir Tamari's *With All Your Possessions* is one of the best resources for understanding the traditional Jewish approach to money, religious practice, and communal life (see "Resources," p. 131).

4. Clifford Goldsmith was a member of Dorshei Tzedek's "Torah of Money" committee. The community of Sek is entirely fictitious, but the story is recreated based on a portion from the Bava Batra tractate of the Babylonian Talmud. In this piece, he uses a traditional Jewish approach to conveying deeper spiritual and ethical matters called *Midrash*. The root of this word in Hebrew is *drash* (to seek out or extrapolate). The classical Midrash is a compilation of sermons, stories, and literary legal discussions of the early rabbis. The idea of using a *midrashic* approach to contemporary Jewish issues has become more popular in the last few years in drama, dance, music, visual art, film, and the written word.

5. These terms are derived from Exodus 30 and 35. You can read the texts in chapter 1 of this book.

6. Jewish and Christian tradition talks about giving tithes and offering. A tithe is understood to be a flat percentage that a person is expected to give, and offerings are "above and beyond" that. Both religions point to texts in the Hebrew Bible when they making a case for tithing, but in practice this evolved from 10 percent of one's produce into a smaller percentage of one's resources.

Epilogue

1. Adapted from Jeffrey Dekro and Lawrence Bush, *Jews, Money and Social Responsibility* (Philadelphia: The Shefa Fund, 1993).

2. Taken from the Jewish Reconstructionist Federation resource book on money and Jewish values, developed initially at a mini-course on Jews, class, and money at the Reconstructionist Rabbinical College, Wyncote, Pennsylvania.

GLOSSARY OF
HEBREW WORDS

Avodah—in biblical and rabbinic context, *Avodah* refers to worship, priestly service in the Temple, Divine service, and parts of Jewish liturgy on Yom Kippur; in Modern Hebrew the word is used for work, labor, and one's profession

B'Tzelem Elohim—derived from Genesis 1:26-27, referring to the creation of human beings in God's image; also refers to a core Jewish value of living an ethical and compassionate life—striving for holiness in one's actions and relationships in the world

Beit Midrash/Beit Knesset—two different terms for a synagogue, the former emphasizing a place of study (from *derash* or "to seek out" or "extrapolate"); the latter emphasizing a place of gathering and convocation

Brit—covenant or pact

Dvar Torah—biblical reference to laws of Torah, contemporarily referring to a sermon, talk, or discussion thematically based on Scripture

Halakha—literally "a way" or "a path"; the legal part of Jewish religious tradition governing all aspects of individual and communal life

Half-Shekel—part of the biblical monetary system; the minimum contribution for upkeep of the Tent of Meeting in the desert and later Temples in Jerusalem

Hevrutah—study partnership; supportive pairing for spiritual inquiry; derived from the word *haver* (friend)

Kabbalah—the corpus of Jewish mystical texts and traditions

L'Shalem—to pay or purchase; from the word *shalom* (peace and wholeness)

Mishkan—the sacred, portable center for the Israelites during the period of desert journeying; derived from the word *shochen* (to dwell) and connected to an experience of God's immanent presence: *shechinah*

Mishnah—compilation of Rabbinic laws, sayings, and thought from roughly 200 BCE to 200 CE

Mitzvah—a commandment or sense of being commanded; an imperative; an action in accordance with Jewish law and custom

Nadiv Lev—freewill offering; an open-hearted gift

O'hel Mo'ed—the Tent of Meeting (see *Mishkan*)

Parnaseem—officials who had the responsibility for collection of *tzedakah*, local taxes, and their distribution within the Jewish community and with the larger governing authorities during the Middle Ages

Shemitah—the biblical practice of leaving parts of a farmed field fallow once every seven years to allow the soil to renew itself

Talmud—combination of the *Mishnah* and the *Gemarah* (rabbinic commentary on the *Mishnah* that includes legal discussions, homilies, stories, and philosophical debates) compiled from about 200 CE to 500–700 CE; the Talmud exists in two versions, one compiled in Babylonia, the other in Palestine

Tanakh—acronym for Torah (five books of Moses), *Nevi'im* (prophets) and *Kituvim* (writings) that comprise the Hebrew Bible

Tishrei—first month of the Jewish calendar that contains the holy days of *Rosh Hashanah* (Jewish New Year), *Yom Kippur* (Day of Atonement), and *Sukkot* (Feast of Booths), usually occurring in September and October

Tikkun HaNefesh—the balancing or repair of the soul; Kabbalistic idea of aligning one's physical, emotional, intellectual, and spiritual life in harmony with the Divine

Tikkun Olam—the renewal and repair of the world; Kabbalistic idea of righting imbalances in the world, in accordance with the principles of *Tikkun HaNefesh;* in the last century it became synonymous with social justice and social action

Tzedakah—the philosophy and proscribed ethical conduct around money in Jewish life based on concepts of justice, compassion, and acting in a godly way with material and financial resources

Yovel—The biblical Jubilee year that was meant to occur after each 49-year cycle. All land and belongings that had been loaned to another were returned to their original owner on the fiftieth year as an acknowledgment of the Divine ownership of all wealth and resources; while outlined in the Bible, the reality of the Jubilee taking place is not clear

RESOURCES

Most Jewish denominations and major Jewish organizations have produced resources to deal with money and congregational life. These include the United Synagogue of Conservative Judaism, the Union of Reform Judaism, the Jewish Reconstructionist Federation, the Center for Leadership and Learning, the Jewish Funders Network, and the Shefa Fund.

BOOKS

The following books have also been helpful for me in my work, along with a wide array of books on money and congregational life published by the Alban Institute.

Altman, Rabbi Remi, ed. *Money Matters: Compassionate Guidelines*. New York: Union for Reform Judaism, 1998.

Amsel, Nachum. *The Jewish Encyclopedia of Moral and Ethical Issues*. Northvale, N.J.: Jason Aronson Inc., 1996.

Bonder, Rabbi Nilton. *The Kabbalah of Money*. Boston: Shambhala Press, 1996.

Breton, Denise, and Christopher Largent. *The Soul of Economies*. Wilmington, Del.: Idea House Publishers, 1991.

Brill, Hal, Jack A. Brill, and Cliff Feigenbaum. *Investing with Your Values: Making Money and Making a Difference*. Princeton, N.J.: Bloomberg Press, 1999.

Buxbaum, Yitzhak. *Jewish Spiritual Practices*. Northvale, N.J.: Jason Aronson Inc., 1990.

Chappell, Tom. *The Soul of a Business*. New York: Bantam Books, 1993.

DeFoore, Bill, and John Renesch, eds. *Rediscovering the Soul of Business*. San Francisco: HarperSanFrancisco, 1995.

Dekro, Jeffrey. *The Highest Degree of Tzedakah: A Guide to Institutional Investment in Low-Income Community Development*. Philadelphia: The Shefa Fund, 1997.

Dekro, Jeffery, and Betsy Tessler. *Building Community, Creating Justice: A Guide for Organizing Tzedakah Collectives*. Philadelphia: The Shefa Fund, 1994.

Dekro, Jeffrey, and Lawrence Bush. *Jews, Money, and Social Responsibility*. Philadelphia: The Shefa Fund, 1993.

Dorff, Rabbi Elliot N. *To Do the Right and Good*. Philadelphia: Jewish Publication Society, 2002.

Edles, L. Peter. *Fundraising: Hands-on Tactics for Non-Profit Groups*. New York: McGraw-Hill, 1993.

HeChasid, Rabbi Yehudah. *Sefer Chasidim*. Trans. Avraham Finkel. Northvale, N.J.: Jason Aronson Inc., 1997.

Hotchkiss, Dan. *Ministry and Money: A Guide for Clergy and Their Friends*. Bethesda, Md.: The Alban Institute, 2002.

Ibn Pakuda, Bachya, *Duties of the Heart*. Trans. Yaakov Feldman. Northvale, N.J.: Jason Aronson Inc., 1996.

Kaplan, Rabbi Mordecai M. *The Future of the American Jew*. New York: MacMillan, 1948.

———. *Judaism as a Civilization*. Philadelphia: Jewish Publication Society, 1934.

Kinder, George. *The Seven Stages of Money Maturity*. New York: Delacorte Press, 1999.

Kravitz, Leonard, and Kerry Olitzky. *Pikre Avot: A Modern Commentary on Jewish Ethics*. New York: UAHC Press, 1993.

Levine, Aaron. *Free Enterprise and Jewish Law: Aspects of Jewish Business Ethics*. KTAV Publishing, New York, 1980.

Needelman, Jacob. *Money and the Meaning of Life*. New York: Doubleday, 1991.

Neusner, Jacob. *The Economics of the Mishnah*. Chicago: University of Chicago Press, 1990.

Pava, Moses. *Business Ethics: A Jewish Perspective*. New York: KTAV Publishing, 1997.

Ronsvalle, John, and Sylvia Ronsvalle. *At Ease: Discussing Money and Values in Small Groups*. Bethesda, Md.: Alban Institute, 1998.

Saperstein, David, and Albert Vorspan. *Tough Choices*. New York: URJ Press, 1992.

Shapira, Rabbi Kalonymus Kalman. *Conscious Community: A Guide to Inner Work.* Trans. Andrea Cohen-Kiener. Northvale, N.J.: Jason Aronson Inc., 1996.

Shapiro, Rabbi Rami M. *Minyan: Ten Practices for Living a Life with Integrity.* New York: Bell Tower, 1997.

Siegel, Danny, *Gym Shoes and Irises: Personalized Tzedakah,* 2 vols. Spring Valley, N.Y.: Town House Press, 1982, 1988.

Tamari, Meir. *The Challenge of Wealth.* Northvale, N.J.: Jason Aronson Inc., 1995.

———. *In the Marketplace: Jewish Business Ethics,* Targum, Mich., 1991.

———. *With All Your Possessions.* Northvale, N.J.: Jason Aronson Inc., 1998.

Teutsch, Dr. David A., *Guide to Jewish Practice: Tsedaka.* Philadelphia: RRC Press, 2005.

Waskow, Arthur. *Down to Earth Judaism: Food, Money, Sex, and the Rest of Life.* New York: William Morrow and Co., 1995.

Yeskel, Felice. "Beyond the Taboo: Talking About Class," in *The Narrow Bridge: Jewish Views on Multiculturalism.* Marla Brettschneider, ed. New Brunswick, N.J.: Rutgers University Press, 1996.

Zevit, Rabbi Shawn Israel, and Shira Stutman. *Money, Values and Your Community: Leadership Curriculum.* Elkins Park, Pa.: Reconstructionist Press, 2004.

ORGANIZATIONS

ALEPH (ALLIANCE FOR JEWISH RENEWAL)

7000 Lincoln Dr. #B2
Philadelphia, PA 19119-3046
(215) 247-0210
www.aleph.org

AMERICAN JEWISH WORLD SERVICE

45 W 36th St.
New York, NY 10018-7904
(212) 736-2597
www.ajws.org

CENTER FOR LEADERSHIP AND LEARNING (CLAL)

440 Park Ave. S, 4th Floor
New York, NY 10016-8012
(212) 779-3300
www.clal.org

JEWISH FUND FOR JUSTICE

330 Seventh Ave., Suite 1401
New York, NY 10001
(212) 213-2113
www.jfjustice.org

JEWISH FUNDERS NETWORK

330 Seventh Ave., 18th Floor
New York, NY 10001
(212) 726-0177
www.jfunders.org

THE JEWISH RECONSTRUCTIONIST FEDERATION (JRF)

7804 Montgomery Ave., Suite 9
Elkins Park, PA 19027
(215) 782-8500
www.jrf.org

NEW ISRAEL FUND NATIONAL OFFICE

1101 14th St. NW, 6th Floor
Washington, DC 20005
(202) 842-0900
www.newisraelfund.org

THE SHALOM CENTER

6711 Lincoln Dr.
Philadelphia, PA 19119
(215) 844-8494
www.shalomctr.org

THE SHEFA FUND

8459 Ridge Ave.
Philadelphia, PA 19128
(215) 483-4004
www.shefafund.org

UNION FOR REFORM JUDAISM (URJ)

633 Third Ave.
New York, NY 10017-6778
(212) 650-4000
www.urj.org

UNITED JEWISH COMMUNITIES

Old Chelsea Station
PO Box 30
New York, NY 10113
(212) 284-6500
www.ujc.org

UNITED SYNAGOGUES OF CONSERVATIVE JUDAISM

155 Fifth Ave.
New York, NY 10010-6802
(212) 533-7800
www.uscj.org